YOUR HOLLYWOOD
PRO

How to Make it in the Movie
Business Without Selling Out

JOHN C. HALL

For information contact:
Retinue Media LLC.
http://yourhollywoodpro.com/

ISBN: 978-0-692-28157-4 - hardcover
ISBN: 978-0-692-28156-7 - eBook

Library of Congress Control Number: 2014949438

Contents

Contents

Foreword

WHEN JOHN asked me to write the foreword to his book, I was of course honored. But I was also apprehensive. I knew it would be hard for me to relate my true feelings about John without sounding so over-the-top and effusive in my praise that people would assume we were related or that he had paid me to wax eloquently about his greatness.

I first met John back in the nineties, when we were both new to the industry and—speaking for myself—about as green as you can get. John now has twenty-plus years in the business. This longevity is as good a measure of a person's professionalism as any other, particularly in Hollywood, which has an almost Darwinian way of weeding out the weaker members of the herd. You have to be tenacious and relentless to make it in this town, and more so to hold on to any success that does come your way. John embodies both of these qualities.

Beyond that, what makes John so singular is his duality: He is both the consummate professional and a true gentleman. This is, if I may be so bold as to suggest, the secret to his continued success. He is a kindhearted person who can still swim with the sharks.

Now there is a stereotype that Hollywood is inhabited exclusively by ruthless go-getters willing to do anything to rise through the ranks and straight into a beach house in Malibu. This reputation is sometimes deserved, sometimes earned, and most often exaggerated.

What makes John so unique is that his passion, his drive if you will, comes from an organic and innate love of the movie business, not some shallow need to get ahead or desire for remuneration. He loves movies, and this has a materially positive effect on his comportment. Anyone who's ever met John can attest to the fact that he literally glows with warmth and positivity. This guy really loves what he does—and it shows.

"So what?" you may be cynically wondering. Lots of people love what they do. What makes Mr. Hall so bloody special? Okay, fine. Fair enough—skepticism has its place.

Let me expound, though: It's the little things that make a man like John great.

Allow me to provide a personal example. Almost every year, John and I (along with other well-meaning members of the industry) attend the Young Variety Day at the Races, a horse-racing charity event at the Santa Anita Racetrack. One year, my mom—her name is Mary, and she's a person who wouldn't miss a chance to bet an inheritance on the ponies—accompanied me to this event. When I introduced her to John, he practically rolled out the red carpet for her. He embraced her with a hug and with a palpable sense of respect. My mother came alive during their conversation, just lit right up, and to this day she still asks me about him. Now my mother is not in the industry, but he treated her like she was genuinely important to him and it showed. That's just John. There is nothing fake or contrived about him. That's simply who he is.

For those who don't know him well, his gentle demeanor may seem to belie his professionalism, but nothing could be further from the truth. It would be a mistake to confuse his kindness with weakness or naïveté. John understands the business side of Hollywood inside and out. He represents studios with aplomb, he understands the people he works with and for, and he knows how to handle himself around both clients and colleagues.

For all of these reasons, he is perhaps one of the most well-regarded and well-respected people in the industry. There's a rare consensus on John C. Hall. Colleagues and competitors alike respect him as both a person and a professional. When John's name comes up, people have only positive things to say. I've never heard one bad word about him, and that's kind of rare, because in Hollywood, everyone talks.

A few years back, John won the Al Shapiro Distinguished Service Award at ShowEast—a prestigious award honoring executives in the motion picture industry. A video testimonial was screened at the award ceremony, and months beforehand they did an open call for anyone who wanted to speak about John, both personally and professionally. I showed up to the office where they were filming the video testimonials and couldn't believe my eyes. There were people lined up out the door like it was a casting call for a major motion picture!

The video was a smashing success, with everyone relating funny stories and loving anecdotes about John. (We also roasted and razzed him for good measure.) That all of these very busy people took time out of their crazy schedules—in the middle of a weekday, no less—to honor John is the greatest testimonial of all. It speaks volumes about the kind of person he is and the respect that his peers have for him.

So have I been too effusive with my praise? Too glowing in my assessment of John? Probably. Do you trust me anyway? I sure hope so. I can't imagine a better adviser and consultant for people entering the industry than John. When I heard he was writing *Your Hollywood Pro* and launching his online portal, YourHollywoodPro.com, both of which aim to help people break into the industry, I just thought, Of course! John. This. Yes! Yes, this makes *perfect sense.*

— *Paul Dergarabedian*
Veteran Movie Industry Analyst

PART I

You Can Make It in Hollywood

1

Stop Starving and Start Opening Doors

"No one conquers who doesn't fight."
—Gabriel Biel

THE RECOGNITION of one's true calling, like all great passions in life, starts with a spark of inspiration. This is true of most fields and interests, and it is certainly true for the entertainment industry—an industry fueled by passion and creativity. Whether your calling is acting, directing, cinematography, or simply the desire to be involved in the entertainment world, you can likely recall the incident or force that first drew you to the industry. It is also likely that this incident continues pushing you forward in the industry even now.

If you have felt this spark, you know just how powerful of an impulse it can be. If you've felt it about the entertainment industry, you probably also understand what it means to be passionate about this field. Your drive is born of a genuine interest in one of the many disciplines in the film industry.

That genuine interest is key to your success. I will be frank with you: this is not an easy business to make it in. If job security means more to you than pursuing your dreams, think long and hard before going into the entertainment industry. There's nothing wrong with wanting job security and a more defined career track. But for some of us, the thrill and artistry of making movies is too powerful a draw.

This book is aimed at those who fall into this latter camp—people who want to break into the entertainment industry, or perhaps those who have already broken in and now want to advance up the career ladder. To make this happen, you will need not only talent but also perseverance and a strong work ethic. To make it in such a competitive industry, you really do need that genuine, driving interest, or you will burn out. A desire for fame or money won't sustain you, for these things are elusive and often fleeting.

Fame and money *might* materialize over time, but they also might not. I urge you to think of real success in terms of the fulfillment of your passion and calling. If you aren't in it for a love of the art and business, there is a good chance you won't stick it out when things get hard, as they almost always do.

Dispel any belief in the myth of the "overnight sensation." There's no such thing, certainly not in such a competitive industry. Tom Cruise, Meryl Streep, Spike Lee, Johnny Depp, and anyone and everyone else who has experienced even a modicum of success in the industry has worked hard to get where they are. For the newest generation of stars, work ethic and dedication is possibly even more important. Many stars start very young. Taylor Lautner was acting practically before he could talk. This doesn't mean you can't start down the path to your dreams later in life; it just means that you have to be ready to travel the long road ahead of you.

Success stories don't just happen—they are made. You have to get down in the trenches, put in the work, and pay your dues. If you just want to make money, don't go into the entertainment industry. Go get an MBA in finance or a law degree, or start a business—do anything else! But if you have that spark and genuine passion for the entertainment world, and you're willing to put in the work, do read on. You will find both camaraderie and counsel in this book.

• • •

So you feel the spark. You're ready to work. If you are really serious, you have probably already been working toward your goals by practicing your craft. Maybe you've taken acting classes or volunteered at a film festival or starred in college productions. These are all great beginning moves—but they're not the only factors that will dictate your success. It's not all about your craft. The entertainment business is a *business*. So if you have already started honing your craft, it is time to start thinking about how to get involved in the industry.

You can't wait for your career to happen to you. You have to make it happen. That means getting out there and actively pursuing a career path. The entertainment field is very different from most industries in that there are innumerable ways to ascend to success. There is no typical career path in Hollywood. Many are lateral, or looping, or undulating. This can be scary, but it also means that you have options, different ladders you can climb as you make your way through the field. The key to finding the right path for you is using the right tools. This book will give you those tools—or tell you where to find them—and teach you how to use them.

The most important tool that you will employ in your rise through Hollywood will be other people. This does not mean you will "use" people, but that you will collaborate, communicate, and network your way to the top—all of which will be explained in intimate detail in this book. The single most poignant realization I have come to after twenty years in show business is that forming and maintaining relationships is paramount to success in Hollywood. When I first started in the field, I had very little experience and no real connections, but the more work I did and the more people I met, the more things began to happen for me. Success snowballs from success, but it all starts by forging connections and gaining experience.

I only wish I had known at the beginning of my career what I know now. That is why I decided to write the book you hold in your hands. I wanted to create a compendium of resources, tools, strategies, and knowledge that would help people more easily forge and navigate their own paths while avoiding as many road bumps as possible, or at least not letting these bumps throw them off track for good.

There's no single secret to success, but there are many things you can do to help advance your career. One is, as I have said, to build relationships—and build them the right way. Another is to narrow your focus and avoid "multihyphenating"; in other words, don't just dabble in multiple areas before you've really laid the groundwork. In the early stages of your career, when you're new and the industry doesn't yet know you, you'll be hired to do one job. You'll be an actor, say, rather than as an actor-director-producer-screenwriter; the other titles can come later, after you've established yourself as an outstanding actor. Identify what you're both good at and thrilled by—and then pursue it with all you've got.

Don't get discouraged, and above all, never give up. The entertainment business is a notoriously tricky field to break into, but people do it all of the time; otherwise, there would be no movies, no studios, no Hollywood. Even the biggest stars are just regular people who kept working until they reached their dream.

Don't let the difficulty discourage you, and definitely don't let other people do so. Your peers, friends, or even family may tell you that you can't make it or that if you haven't become an "overnight sensation" by now, you'll never be a sensation at all. Throughout the first half of my life and the early years of my career, I heard the same thing. It's frustrating, and it's hard to believe in yourself enough to do the work when others don't believe in you.

Understand this, though: When someone isn't successful in Hollywood, the reason is never because they *can't* do it. It's because they *won't* do it, or they *didn't* do it. They chose not to—or simply didn't choose to stick with it. You have to commit and give it your absolute all. You've got to find that drive that enables you to believe in yourself and your dreams, even when others think those dreams are foolhardy. You have to roll up your sleeves and fight to make it happen. No one is going to do it for you.

Everyone's situation is different, and no success stories are exactly the same. As we explore some of the tools and resources that can help jump-start your career, consider your own situation. Which tools and strategies are most relevant to your needs?

How can you position yourself to take advantage of the resources around you? There are resources everywhere if you know where to look, especially in the age of the Internet.

This book will cover a variety of topics, but it's in no way exhaustive. As we delve into specifics on how to network, where to live, and what other steps to take to become a Hollywood pro yourself, don't hesitate to reach out to professionals for advice and to seek out other content that can inspire you and help you along the way.

2

Inciting Incidents: How I Got Started (And How You Can, Too!)

WHILE IT is true that everyone must forge their own path in Hollywood, that doesn't mean you can't learn from others— indeed, learning from others is exactly what you must do. Seek out successful people in the industry and find out their stories. Ask them about their experiences, what worked for them, and how they got where they are today. There is something to learn from everyone in the industry—even me. To that end, what follows is the story of how I got started in the industry.

Let me begin by saying that I had no contacts in the entertainment industry when I started out. My parents were not famous, and we lived nowhere close to Hollywood. I grew up in a small town outside Louisville, Kentucky. My dad owned a card and gift shop downtown in a local shopping mall. It was not unusual for me to go with him after a long day of work (for him) and school (for me) to help with the business. I helped take the trash out to the dumpster and count the daily take, and if I was lucky, I might get to turn the key to lock the door for the night.

To be blunt, my father's shop did not excite me. It was a regular retail business, complete with cash registers, not-so-thrilling merchandise, and a whole lot of number crunching and inventory counting. I was bored to tears every time he dragged me to work with him. He was probably trying to train me to take over the family business and follow in his footsteps. Or maybe he just wanted to instill an entrepreneurial spirit in me. Whatever his reasons, I was not interested. The shop was all fine and good for someone who wanted to run a store, but it didn't ignite that spark of passion in me.

The one upside to going to the shop was that it was next door to a Radio Shack. Once we closed up shop in the evening, I'd wander next door to look at the latest and greatest television sets, glowing just across the way. This was in the early 1980s—there were no sleek flat-screen TVs, just the big, chunky tube televisions of yore. There was no satellite cable either, just what the TV could pick up via rabbit-ear antennas.

The manager of this particular Radio Shack always kept the sets tuned to the same station. On one particular evening, the TVs were showing a network special that caught my attention: *The Making of "Raiders of the Lost Ark."* Ten-year-old me sat transfixed as all the mysteries of this movie were revealed before my eyes. I had liked the film, but that wasn't what enthralled me. What captured my imagination was my very first look at the filmmaking process.

As a kid, I used to think movies were made very simply: Somebody turned on a camera, and all the events unfolded right then and there. I understood that there were costumes and actors, but it had never quite registered that there were hundreds of other people and jobs involved. Everything was staged, special effects had to be employed, and the magic wasn't really magic.

Watching the *Making of "Raiders"* special, I was fascinated, and I suddenly realized that this was a job. People worked to create cinematic stories, just like my dad worked to run his business or the Radio Shack manager worked to close his store each night. Somewhere, somehow, making movies was a job that people actually got paid for, and at that moment, I realized that this was what I wanted to do for a living.

That was my inciting incident. There were certainly many other crucial moments later in life, but this split second of understanding that it took actual live people doing actual paid work to make movies is when my love of the industry began, and it is what continues to push me forward today. I knew then, for the first time, that this was what I wanted to do.

Some people figure it out while acting onstage in a school play, others when they're seeing a movie for the first time and can't take their eyes off the screen. Some know when they're ten, and some know when they're thirty or older, but we all share this type of moment that drives us to work and keeps us in the business through thick and thin.

Not long after I saw the *Making of "Raiders"* special, *Star Wars: Return of the Jedi* was released in theaters. Having already seen the first two *Star Wars* movies, I was determined to see this one the day it came out. I knew I'd have to get out of school early, and my dad, seeing how important it was to me, wrote me a phony note to give to the school's secretary. The note claimed that my grandparents were visiting from out of town and wanted to spend time with me.

It was, of course, a complete lie; my grandparents lived in town, and I saw them all of the time. But my grandfather did take me to the movie. My grandmother wanted no part of it, but my grandfather, who had stories of seeing the picture shows in the twenties and thirties, agreed to drive me downtown to Showcase Cinema. On that spring day in 1983, he picked me up and off we drove.

My grandfather had no idea what he was getting himself into. I hadn't explained to him that we were going to see the third movie of a trilogy, because I thought he might not take me if he knew he hadn't seen the first two movies. When we pulled up to the theater, the line was already wrapped around the block—a literal blockbuster.

My eyes went wide as we walked in. There were copies of the movie book being sold at the concession stand and fans dressed up as characters. News channels were documenting the spectacle. Camera flashes fired off like strobe lights. As my grandfather and I sat down in the theater with our popcorn, a woman dressed as Princess Leia walked in, followed, of course, by cameras.

"Who is that?" my grandfather whispered to me.

"She's the princess," I said.

He looked puzzled. "The princess of what?" he said, incredulously.

"She's the princess of the movie!" I said, exasperated. It was then, though, that it occurred to me just how affecting movies could be. Movies, perhaps more than any other narrative medium, brought characters and stories to life. Even as a kid in middle school, I understood how powerful this medium could be. Not everyone gets it—in this case my grandfather didn't—but I sure did connect with the audience experience that day.

Attending the premiere with my grandfather also gave me another look at all of the jobs involved in making movies happen. There was an element of exhibition that until now, I hadn't witnessed. There were ushers with flashlights and ticket-takers and people selling popcorn—all jobs involved in the craft of movie magic. So many people were employed and engaged for the sole purpose of making this movie work. I was astounded.

Once my parents saw how important the cinematic world was to me—I literally skipped school to see *Star Wars!*—they quietly decided to begin nurturing this passion. My dad dug out his old eight-millimeter camera, and my friends and I started making movies.

Prior to my dad giving me the camera, I had been trying to make movies with my friends without a camera—a doomed endeavor. Most of my friends just wanted to play sports, or Dungeons & Dragons, or Pac-Man video games. None of this really interested me. I had a singular focus from a very young age—what I wanted was to play at making movies. When I went over to my friends' houses, I would sometimes bring costumes and props. I was very into make-believe—always inventing some plot or struggle to act out. There was always conflict! Orchestrated conflict, to be sure, but it was there. I just wished I could capture it on film. Sometimes other kids would get annoyed with me directing them—they just wanted to play make-believe, but I wanted to tell a story. I had to cajole them into playing along.

Things got better for me on this front after my dad gave me his old camera. Suddenly, my friends were really into it and we began videotaping our movies. It was really a lot like the 2011 movie *Super 8*, where the kids are determined to create great cinema with whatever tools are at hand. My friends and I would come up with elaborate story lines, and we'd go out scouting for locations. We didn't have any training whatsoever; everything we knew, we learned from the making-of specials that continued to crop up on television. We just mimicked the people we saw on the specials and made our own movies. When we finished filming, we'd set up in someone's basement and invite all of our friends and family over for a viewing. The movies were only a few minutes long, and they were cheesy, and they didn't have sound (my eight-millimeter couldn't record it), but they were ours.

The more serious I got with my filmmaking, the more my parents supported me. In eighth grade, I created the Young Movie Producers' Club, which I used as a vehicle to get word out about my projects with the eight-millimeter. I wrote scripts on legal pads and started using my middle initial in my stage name—because "John Hall" was my grandfather, not me. With the approach of the video age, my father went out and got me the first camera of my very own, which I'm sure at that time cost him upwards of one thousand dollars. It was a great camera, and I loved him for it.

Now that I finally had a camera that could capture sound, I learned pretty quickly that I could record things for people—for pay! I was young enough that I didn't quite know what to charge, but I understood that the camera had been expensive. I arbitrarily settled on forty dollars an hour, and set to work building my new business.

Recording events like weddings, birthday parties, graduations, and other celebrations for money was just a new business model, and I was lucky enough to get in on the ground floor. Another stroke of luck: By this point, my father's greeting card store had become a small chain—and where better to advertise for the filming of weddings, birthday parties, and graduations than at a card store that catered to weddings, birthday parties, and graduations? My dad became my biggest promoter and source of new clients. He had his employees distribute business cards that I printed out. He dutifully posted fliers and let me leave them on the counter next to the register. My parents dropped me off and picked me up from gigs, because I didn't have a driver's license.

Even as a young teenager, capturing the images—and emotions—of families and friends during some of the happiest days of their lives left me with an indescribable feeling. I can vividly remember shooting at a woman's ninetieth birthday party and how alive it made me feel. I loved the job I'd created for myself, and I thought I wanted to do it forever. I'd fallen in love with the cameras and the magic of film.

As you can see, my passion for the business of entertainment—and not just the craft—started relatively early on. These formative moments and experiences were the building blocks for me, the foundation on which I based my entire career. I grew from a young kid watching network TV specials in Kentucky into an executive and producer in Hollywood, and as I look back on my life, I can identify every moment, good and bad, that brought me to where I am now.

It takes some people longer to find exactly what they want out of life, but the urge and the drive is all the same, and it's an urge and a drive to follow. I was lucky to know exactly where I wanted to be at so young an age, but you don't have to have a videotaping business and a TV show (more on that later) under your belt before you turn twenty-one, as I did. As long as you have the passion and you're willing to do the work to pursue it, you can get there.

3

Stop Talking Yourself Out of Pursuing Your Dream

EVERYONE IS a critic. We all have opinions, and most of us aren't hesitant to share them. Everyone wants to be the coach in the bleachers, the backseat driver, the sports analyst, the magazine columnist. And nowhere is this more true than in Hollywood, where there's an entire industry designed solely to critique the entertainment business and scrutinize celebrities. There are the actual critics, who write or produce reviews, and there are the shows, like *TMZ*, that follow the everyday lives of stars yet don't even begin to touch on their professional work. And then there are websites where laymen can praise or scorn to their heart's content. People share their opinions offline, too, talking about celebrities and movies in hair salons, restaurants, and bars all around the world.

Hollywood is a dream factory for everyone, not just for those who want to work in the industry. The public's fascination with movies and movie stars is born of a vicarious desire to be a part of their world. At some point in life, nearly everyone dreams of becoming a star (regardless of actual plans to pursue the dream). Everyone wants to have a beautiful person's life, to have fame and fortune, to travel the world. We are enamored with the glamorous life.

Unfortunately, this means that those of us who do pursue the dream and make it are under constant scrutiny from both the media and the public. All of this attention can make us super-sensitive to criticism, and even to comments that aren't actually negative. Other actors may say things like, "Oh, you didn't get the part," and other filmmakers might make remarks like, "Ah, your short didn't get admitted into the film festival." These may be genuine expressions of sympathy, but they can seem like thinly veiled personal digs.

Even when you're riding high, you might receive (or perceive) negativity from others. You might be cast in a movie, only to be left on the cutting room floor (which has become a very common turn of phrase and phenomenon). Or you produced a film, but "it's too bad" that you don't have script approval or final cut rights.

You hear this kind of negativity all the time, and you imagine it just as often. There is no escaping the specter of criticism in an industry that is under constant scrutiny, be it from professionals, peers, or just ordinary people. There is a plus side to this—constructive criticism is the primary vehicle for collaboration—but it can definitely be a downer to feel so perpetually watched and judged. The only thing you can do, though, is steel yourself against the inevitable negativity. Ready yourself to face criticism, and don't allow it to stop or discourage you.

You also need to prepare yourself for rejection. Find a way to cope with it, because it's going to come, and it's going to come in many forms and fashions. That's the nature of ultra-competitive industries. A delicate soul may be good for your art, but you'll need a thick skin to shield yourself from the onslaught of rejection. It's unfortunate, but part of the business. And you don't have the time to let criticism and rejection get you down. You have to dust yourself off and get back in the game. Don't take the rejection of a project, a role, or an application as a rejection of your entire career. Every single person who has become successful has been rejected many times in their lives and will be again before all is said and done.

Be it a rejection letter, a nasty comment from a casting director, or a mordant review, you cannot allow it to derail your dreams. Learn how to take rejection and criticism graciously. The best way is to practice. Get your work out there and get some bad reviews! Get yourself some of that "thanks, but no thanks." Get some rejection letters on your script and stick them on your fridge so you can laugh at them the day your script sells! In the meantime, ask friends and peers for honest appraisals of your work. Criticism will follow you through your entire career, no matter how successful you become, so build up a tolerance now.

Don't succumb to self-doubt. With input coming from peers, potential employers, columnists, bloggers, and anyone and everyone who thinks they know their way around a movie, it's easy to become your own worst critic as a proactive measure to soften the blow of bad feedback. This can be paralyzing to your career. If you're not careful (and sometimes even if you are), you can talk yourself out of your dream before you have the chance to succeed.

Leave the criticism to the critics. Don't beat yourself up just because they sometimes do. But do use criticism to your advantage—learn how to learn from it. Analyze your own work, but be constructive, not destructive. Ask yourself, How can I do better? Not, how am I failing?

In college, I started a TV show called *Lights Out* with a group of friends I'd made in a television club. We worked on the show for the better part of a year, and to our delight, we got it up and running on a real TV superstation airing across the whole region. We were on a whirlwind, and I thought, "This is it. This is the beginning of my career, and I'm not even at legal drinking age yet. I'm the associate producer on a TV show, and I'm going places."

Of course, as soon as I'd settled into this new reality, disaster struck. My friends and I had been working with some people at Fox in order to get the show on network television. Fox was a fledgling network at the time, and the guy who was pushing for our show got replaced by an executive who didn't want anything to do with it. We were pretty much kicked to the curb.

I felt like my life had been derailed. I had convinced myself that *Lights Out* was my one and only shot, and I fell into a very dark place. Self-doubt took over, and I started to believe my own bad press. I began to think the naysayers were right—and to wonder if this was really the business for me.

Meanwhile, I was graduating from college. My friends and I now had to go out and find other jobs—real jobs in the real world. I ended up working at a restaurant and a video store. I even spent time working at my father's gift shop. I found these jobs demoralizing but, perhaps paradoxically, they slowly ignited the passion in me to get back to my Hollywood dream.

I called up a contact I had made from a previous internship and asked if he could find me anything in the entertainment industry. He didn't have any good Hollywood leads, and instead ended up referring me to one of his clients, a tech company that made power inverters. Don't ask me what a power inverter is—I didn't know then and I don't know now. Still, the owner of this small start-up offered me a job in sales. I had no passion for sales, but I realized I could at least earn more doing sales than working at the gift shop or video store. So I took the job.

My job was to cold-call clients. I was spectacularly bad at this, probably because I didn't really know what we were selling or care to learn. I didn't like the job, but it paid okay, which was more than I could say for the video store.

Money, or the lack thereof, can be a powerful motivator, of course. My new boss had founded the business after quitting an engineering job with Motorola. He had worked out how much money he would make at his Motorola job based on salary projections. The number scared him—so he quit right away and started the business selling power inverters. He never looked back.

I did this same exercise one day at the office while eating lunch at my desk. I calculated how much money I would make if I sold as many power inverters as I could every day for the rest of my life. What I found was the opposite of what my boss had found at Motorola—the number wasn't bad. It was a lot more money than I had ever made before. Unfortunately, this did not make me feel better. The number I focused on wasn't preceded by the dollar sign. I kept staring at the number of power inverters I would need to sell. I started thinking of the years and years it would take to do this and I slumped down into my chair, terribly depressed.

My mind went back to the Radio Shack. I remembered the *Making of "Raiders"* special. I thought about *Lights Out. Oh, my god*, I asked myself, *what am I doing here?* I knew then that this was not only a life I didn't want, but it was robbing me of the one I desired. I had to find a way back into the world of entertainment.

I worked that job for exactly nine months before I got back on course. The experience taught me a lot—namely that "real jobs" weren't for me and that I belonged in the entertainment business. I discovered that working a typical nine-to-five wouldn't make me happy. I knew because I had tried! I had a good job, good hours, good pay, and good benefits, but at the end of the day, I just wasn't where I wanted to be.

If you're waking up every day and forcing yourself to do something that you don't like doing, it's time to reevaluate your career path. And maybe it's time to get back to pursuing your dream. Working some corporate or retail job you don't have a passion for might be just the push you need. It's good to explore your options in life, as long as you make sure you don't get sidetracked for too long. You need to be sure that what you are doing is really getting you where you want to go. You don't want to wake up one day and realize that you have been on the wrong journey after you have already reached the destination. If something isn't working and you know it, change course. Ditch that "real job" and get back to your real life's work.

If you stay in the wrong job too long, you might start to feel more and more stuck. Some people hit a low point, like I did with *Lights Out*, and decide to get a real job, but then they never come back. There are also people who give themselves six months in Hollywood to succeed, and tell themselves that they'll give up on their dream if they can't make it in the allotted time.

Why do this to yourself? Why place an arbitrary time limit on perseverance and ambition? The answer is usually self-doubt.

Self-doubt is definitely normal. As an up-and-comer in the entertainment business, you are essentially fated to feel self-doubt at some point. You'll find a way, if only temporarily, to derail your own dream and succumb to the nagging inner voice that tells you, "Okay, this is the end of the road." I'm here to say that it's not the end of the road; it's part of the journey. Don't listen to that little voice—it has a crappy attitude and doesn't know what it's talking about. There are ways to find a job in Hollywood and keep your dream on track.

Tackle your doubts early on. I certainly did. You might find out how willing you are to get back on track and try your hand at the entertainment industry again. But if you find that you have gotten derailed, don't let that stop you. If you've been working at the same unsatisfying job for twenty years and you get the itch to get back into the entertainment business, go for it. It's not too late unless you're dead. You may not be able to outright abandon what you've been working on, but there are ways for you to pursue the dream while maintaining the life you've already created for yourself. You just need to be realistic about your expectations—at any age. At forty or fifty, you may be too old to be a starlet, but you're never too old to be an actor.

Your inciting incident directed you toward a goal for a reason. Whatever that moment was, it was the baseline for finding out what you want to do in life. There's a reason you're good at your passion, and why it comes easily to you. If acting is your thing, you'll figure it out. If it's directing, you'll figure it out. The reason it feels easy is because you enjoy it. If waiting tables doesn't come easily to you, there's a reason—you probably don't enjoy it. There are people who like working in the service industry; you just may not be one of them. If you truly want a career in the entertainment industry, own that. Don't be embarrassed. Lots of people want to work in the entertainment industry—that's why it's called the Hollywood *Dream,* after all. Yes, breaking into the industry can be difficult, but that doesn't make it a pipe dream. Working in Hollywood is a real career like any other.

Learning to ignore your self-doubt is easier said than done, I know. Sometimes you need to fight to keep your head in the right place. If you don't, you can wind up sabotaging yourself. I've seen this happen to my peers as well as my clients—they find ways to give up just as they're getting close to making it. They are so scared of failing that they stop trying.

I once worked with a filmmaker who just kept hitting a wall with a project she was working on. Every time she finished a scene, she insisted that it needed to be reedited. "It just needs one more edit. I just need to do it one more time!" she'd tell me. Once she *finally* completed that scene, she moved onto the next and had the same problem again and then again with the next scene. At the end, when she eventually finished what should have been the final version, she said to me, "I need a full-time professional editor. I don't have the money to hire one, and that's the only thing that's going to make my movie right." She scared herself out of her own dream—she never finished editing because she was afraid of what people might say when they saw the final product.

You need to have courage and conviction in your work, no matter what it is. Don't obsess over the performance, the editing, the lighting…don't trick yourself into endless tinkering and tampering. Revision is the most important part of the writing process, but revision can also be a means of procrastination. Be prepared to commit to crossing the finish line. I see people abandon projects prematurely all of the time. I see them do it with their entire careers, too. You may be talking yourself out of pursuing your dream simply because you're afraid of what you'll do once you obtain it.

Persistence in your endeavors will also help you stave off self-doubt. Be too busy to second-guess yourself. You won't be able to let the fear of failure talk you out of working if you're too busy working to be bothered by fear.

If you feel stalled out and uninspired, look to the work of others to get you back on track. Go to a movie and remind yourself why you want to be involved in the business. Go to that play, that comedy show, that revival of an old classic. You'll absorb rich content while in the company of like-minded people; some of them may even long to be in the industry, too. Immersing ourselves in the things we love about film can help us rekindle our passion for it.

If you want to be doing something, you need to go do it. It sounds so simple, but working somewhere else and telling yourself that you'll get to the dream anyway won't make things happen for you. I like to draw inspiration from Captain Picard of *Star Trek: The Next Generation*. His most famous catchphrase was, "Engage!" You can't get anywhere without that first engagement. So take Picard's advice: Engage, engage, engage!

One of the very real concerns for people trying to make it in the industry is, "How can I financially support myself and stay engaged in the business?" This is a legitimate question and one that must often be addressed immediately. You won't be going to a lot of auditions if you can't make rent!

Look for a job that will keep you involved in the industry. There are several temp agencies in Los Angeles that can help you find entertainment jobs. If you can't find exactly what you're looking for, get creative. After I quit my "real job," I tore tickets at movie theaters to make a living, and I was constantly surrounded by the industry because of it. If you're in L.A., work at one of the hip movie theaters. The industry is literally right in the lobby waiting for you. You'll absorb content, and what's more, half of your clients will be people in the industry; some of whom you might even recognize. Such theaters are often the site of industry events that, as an employee, you may get to attend.

All too often, I hear an aspiring filmmaker or actor say, "I'll become a waiter or a bartender because they make a few extra bucks in tips." That's fine, but do it on the weekends, or another time when it doesn't conflict with something that'll keep you moving in the business. You still need to find a job that directly engages you with the industry. If you need the extra money to get by, take an unrelated part-time job, but don't let it interfere with your progress in the business.

In the end, you'll eventually have to find a way to get into the business and stay there. It may take time, but keep trying. And don't succumb to self-doubt. Remind yourself that these struggles are normal and part of the process. Remind yourself that others have made it in Hollywood before you, and that you can, too, with persistence and with a lot of engagement.

4

"Engage!" Getting the Best Education Out of the World Around You

WHETHER OR not you go to film school, there are many ways to educate yourself about the industry. And you must continue to educate yourself over the course of your career. Remember Captain Picard's line: "Engage!" Engage in the business and continue absorbing content, and you will learn all you need to know. Film school is of course the most commonly acknowledged form of education, but you don't need a formal education to progress in the industry. As long as you engage and immerse yourself thoroughly, you have a great shot.

In this chapter, I want to talk about some of the more common ways people begin to engage with the industry.

The Truth About Internships

Getting an internship is one of the best ways to prepare yourself for the working world. This is true in all fields and industries, the entertainment business included. Summer internships, gap-year internships, internships that you can complete during the course of the school year—these are all huge assets to you, and a great way to continue your education and begin your career. Internships sometimes turn into jobs, but even if they don't, they can teach you a lot that will make you more employable down the line. Internships are definitely not just for students. In fact, they may be *most* valuable to those who haven't gone to film or acting school, precisely because of the skills you'll learn on the job.

Working for little to no money isn't ideal for your bank account, but it can build your career. Think long-term. No one ever got rich doing internships, but many people have used them to launch careers. An internship can allow you to work at places where you might not have otherwise gotten hired. In this sense, it's almost like taking an extra course or a workshop. Getting a salary-paying job at a big studio or firm takes experience, but these internships can be your tutelage, providing the experience that will get you there.

There are always internships to be found, and the Internet will be your number one resource in finding them. If you're a student, your school may have a career services center that can be of help. Keep your eyes peeled; look at bulletin boards in libraries and peruse journals if you need to. You can find an internship anywhere. I found my first internship on a corkboard at a college bookstore.

For me, that job was with Mark Logan and Associates, a small marketing firm in Texas. Mark Logan was a direct-marketing consultant, and his organization would place ads in grocery store circulars or create commercials for local TV stations. It was the epitome of a "one-man operation"—it was just Logan (and, occasionally, another assistant). This wasn't my dream job, but it wasn't wholly unrelated to my interests either.

Even if the internship you find doesn't seem like a fit, you'll be able to learn from it. Marketing wasn't the direction I wanted to go in professionally, but I found a broadcasting angle to pursue within the position that both interested me and allowed me to hone my media skills. I also learned how to work in an office environment, which is a skill that producers need to have. You'll learn—as I did—how to manage a front desk and how to work a copy machine and other office technology. You can even glean knowledge simply from fetching coffee for someone. Just by being available to do seemingly menial tasks, you can forge relationships.

Don't hesitate to ask questions during your internship. If you're getting coffee for someone, use that opportunity to connect with them. Most people enjoy talking about what they're doing and telling the story of how they got where they are. In any office where you intern, you'll be able to find someone who can share their experience and give you a perspective on how to get where you want to be. In addition to learning these new perspectives, you'll start to forge professional relationships that could be important to you later on in your career.

Use an internship as a way to gain access to people you otherwise wouldn't have access to. Mine their backstories to learn about the industry. And aim to make friends and connections wherever you are. Do be tactful, though. Try not to ask the wrong questions at the wrong times. Pay attention to the cues people throw off through body language, and be mindful of people's time and workspace.

Because internships are short, you need to use your time to really shine. Make a good impression right away and follow through. Establish yourself as an eager, dedicated worker right off the bat. Do your best at all times.

You also want to make a good impression socially. Let your personality and sense of humor shine through in your work; nobody likes a robot, not even a coffee-fetching robot. Buy a mug for yourself or your boss that says, "Get Shit Done!" A gesture like that will help establish your commitment to the job...and your sense of humor. (Beware, though: The worst thing you can do is buy that mug and then *not* get shit done. So don't let your swag betray you! Or rather, don't betray your swag!)

An office environment, regardless of the industry, is a great source of contacts. Ask for business cards, or if you can't get one, write down the names and numbers of everyone you talk to. If you work with assistants or other interns, don't be dismissive; they might become executives or filmmakers one day. There's always a good chance that a relationship might benefit both of you in the future. You never know who will end up where, and you may be able to pull strings with someone later if you first served in the trenches together. One of my former coworkers in an internship ended up working at PBS. I still have her contact information on hand. I never know when I'll need to be in touch with PBS, but when I do, I'll know whom to call.

One of the best things about internships is the access they give you to industry functions like screenings, cocktail parties, fund-raisers—you name it. In the entertainment industry, events pop up all the time, and you should take advantage of them.

Early on in my career, this happened to me almost weekly: The office would get an invitation to a social gathering, and no one who'd been working there for more than a year would want to go. That's where you get to step in as an intern. You can politely offer to attend on behalf of the office. Most people in the office are tired of going to these functions because they happen so frequently, and they'll be more than happy to let you go in their stead.

Don't let the word *nontransferable* on a ticket scare you. This is the one case in the entertainment business where it's appropriate to bend the rules, because it happens all the time, and because that's how you make contacts. We'll talk more about how to navigate these events in Part III of this book, but at this stage, my basic advice is this: Just go. Get yourself out there. You'll meet so many people, and you'll learn simply by observing. It's another phase of your education.

Content Is King

In Hollywood, content is king. There is no dearth of content, and there never will be. I learned this quite intimately while interning at the Tandy Film Library at Texas Christian University. I was the assistant student curator there, and my main task was to catalog the inventory and make sure that all the content was in good shape before we lent it out to the public. I worked there in the library's early years, back in the eighties, which meant that we handled a mass of videotapes and laser discs.

While cataloging the inventory, I had to watch literally every tape that passed through my hands. Over the years, I watched hundreds of movies and TV shows in order to ensure that there were no imperfections on the tapes or discs. Our inventory ranged from MGM's classic musicals to documentaries to every episode of *Star Trek* ever made. I don't mean to romanticize the work. I was certainly bored sometimes— watching fifty back-to-back episodes of *Leave It to Beaver* will do that to you. The curator and my mentor, the late John Freeman, would quiz me about flaws in the tapes and other technical imperfections, and he often had me watch and rewatch things to make sure I was getting it right.

That job was a huge part of my education in film, perhaps more valuable than my film school coursework. If I worked an eight-hour shift, I'd be watching three or four movies in one day. I was exposed to thousands of hours of content—and all of it on the clock! It was like a crash course in the history of cinematography, directorial techniques, aesthetics, and all the other elements of film.

But the number-one thing I learned was just how much content there is out there and how important it is to always be taking it in. Hollywood isn't the only place where movies and shows are shot. There's also New York, London, Tokyo, China, and India, to name just a few. There are literally millions of hours of entertainment content out there, and you can learn from all of it (yes, even from *Leave It to Beaver*).

Behind-the-scenes specials and documentaries are a particularly great way to learn, and today's DVDs and Blu-rays frequently come with such extras. If you are trying to break into the industry now, you have an advantage over those of us who did it in the eighties. You don't have to work in a library. You can find more content online than you would at a film library. Netflix and Hulu are troves of content. And the more content you absorb, the more you'll learn about the industry. It's just a matter of committing to learn it all.

Absorbing content, and especially behind-the-scenes content, will lead you to the same discovery I made when I watched

The Making of "Raiders of the Lost Ark" oh so long ago: There are far more people and jobs involved in filmmaking than just actors and directors. Acting, directing, camera work—these are all just the tip of the iceberg. It takes an army of people to put out a film. There are hundreds of jobs assisting those people, and hundreds of jobs creating special effects, costumes, makeup, music, and more.

Taking in all of this content, you might begin to get different ideas about what you want to do or what you could do to get your foot in the door. You might find a whole new direction to go in. We aren't all born to be actors and filmmakers. Take the time to watch, to learn, to really pay attention, and you are likely to discover, or narrow down, your calling.

Extra Work

A great hands-on way to learn is to take on extra work within the industry, on top of your day job. Agents and acting coaches sometimes advise against this on the grounds that too many side gigs will clutter your résumé, but there's an easy solution: Leave them off your résumé! Nothing can compare with actually being on deck as the cinematic magic happens. It's like watching football from the sidelines—you learn by exposure and observation. Not to mention the added access it provides. If you have an opportunity and the time to take on extra work, doing so will be well worth your while.

It's also a wonderful way to make money. Think of it this way: You could work in a restaurant, or you could spend the day getting paid to be on a movie set. If you already have an office job, take a week's vacation and spend it working on a set. You never know who you'll meet and where those new connections could take you.

If you don't live in Hollywood, you may have to look harder for relevant work, but most large cities have at least some industry jobs. A few agencies advertise on Facebook, and some in newspapers. Put in the time and effort to find a job in the field so that you can make the connections you need. You can't get anywhere with inaction—but if you take that first step, you're on your way.

• • •

Because of the wealth of content and opportunities for engagement out there, anyone can become an expert. You don't have to attend an expensive school—you can if you'd like, but you can also learn what you need from real-world experience. Commit to engaging yourself constantly, both by absorbing content and by working in the industry in any capacity you can, and you will be on the path to success.

PART II

How Hollywood Really Works

5

We're a Company Town, and We're in the Creativity Business, but You Have to Move Here to Make It

AT SOME point in your career, you're going to have to move to a city with a major entertainment industry market. In the United States, this means either Los Angeles or New York. I'm sorry to dash your dreams of country living or small-town charm, but if you want to be a serious contender in the industry, you'll have to relocate to one of these industry hubs. You might be able to retreat to that dream home in Alaska sometime *after* you become wildly successful, but you'll never reach that level of success if you are not physically available to give and get access.

The logistics of the industry require you to be there. The major studios are in these cities. When a director wants you on set for a next-day film shoot, or your agent lands you an eight-week run on Broadway, there is no telecommuting. If you can't be there, they're going to find someone else who can be.

Proximity is also crucial to networking. If you don't maintain a physical presence in one of the major markets, you won't be meeting the right people in the industry. You can't do much networking in small-town America because all of the talent and industry flock to Los Angeles or New York. You can do some, but there's a limit.

In my early twenties, I worked for the Kim Dawson Talent Agency in Dallas. It paid me next to nothing, but it was a good introduction to working with actors. And after cutting my teeth there, I decided to open up a talent agency of my own. I went down to the courthouse and filed papers for Entertainment Industries, the newest agency in town.

Any lofty dreams I had of running a glamorous talent agency were immediately dashed. As it turns out, the entertainment industry didn't need a talent agency run by a college kid in Texas. I listed Entertainment Industries in the yellow pages, but all I ever got were calls to book exotic dancers. This wasn't exactly the kind of talent I was hoping to represent, but in true entrepreneurial fashion, I made the most of the opportunity and spent several months booking exotic dancers for a 10 percent fee. This was all well and good for a little pocket change, but I wanted to work in the movies, not in the strip clubs, so I closed down the agency.

Why did Entertainment Industries fail? The problem wasn't with me; it was with my location. The agency never stood a chance. You can't represent talent that isn't there. The best talent in the area was already represented by Kim Dawson—and anyone better had left for one of the coasts. If I was going to represent them, I was going to have to go there, too.

I'm not saying that you can't lay the foundation for your career in a smaller town; you can, and I am going to explain how in subsequent chapters. But again, eventually you are going to have to live in one of the two major hubs if you want to be taken seriously.

On occasion, small entertainment-industry hubs will spring

up in different cities. A major studio might shoot a film or television show in another city, for the setting or for the tax breaks and lower overhead costs offered there. Such productions can take anywhere from six months to a year or longer, and a cottage industry can spring up around them.

Dallas was a hot spot in the late eighties and early nineties, which is how I got my first job with a major studio. I was then transferred to the Atlanta publicity office to support new filming there. Atlanta was something of a satellite industry city, and still is. *The Hunger Games* and *Fast & Furious 7* were recently shot there. But these kinds of mini-hubs are rare nowadays. Occasionally one will pop up and be hailed the new "third coast," as Atlanta was, and Dallas before that, and Vancouver before that—but it always fizzles out eventually. If you can catch one of these waves, you might be able to use it to launch a career, as I did in Dallas, but none of these satellite markets seem to last. Eventually the scene dries up, the work disappears, and you have to get yourself to a major market.

That said, there are definitely things you can do in smaller towns to lay the foundation for your career. My own life is a testament to this. You can be in local theater productions, maybe do some commercial work, and even get a job with a satellite studio, especially if you live in a major city like Atlanta, Chicago, Philadelphia, or Dallas. But if you want to be a major player in the entertainment industry, you will ultimately have to go to New York or Los Angeles, and there is no good reason to delay. The sooner you get there, the better.

I had made lots of contacts in the industry prior to coming to Los Angeles, but it wasn't until I got there that things really started happening for me. Suddenly, people started taking me more seriously. Shortly after moving to Los Angeles, I was asked to be a juror at a film festival by a contact I had met while working at the studio in Atlanta. But she didn't reach out until I was living in Los Angeles. It was as if she suddenly realized, "Oh, he's *really* in the industry." (I was invited back, and later served on the juries of the Palm Beach International Film Festival and the Santa Barbara International Film Festival multiple times.)

Even though I had run my own small company, produced a TV show for a major network, and worked in a major studio, I didn't get the invites necessary to take me to the next level until I was actually working in Los Angeles. Being in Los Angeles and working at a major Hollywood studio allowed me to cement myself as a contender in the field in a way that working for a major studio in Dallas had not.

When it comes to the industry, Los Angeles and New York lend you a certain gravitas that other places just don't. Working on Broadway is simply more prestigious than working on a theatrical production in a smaller market. Being a producer in Atlanta has different implications than being a producer in Hollywood. It's a geographical prejudice that, like it or not, exists—and for good reason. The caliber of filmmaker or executive that you meet at a West Coast film festival is, generally speaking, higher than that of a filmmaker you will find in another location. The best of the best, and certainly the most high profile, come to Hollywood (or New York City) for the advantages of being here.

And you should, too.

6

In Hollywood, Everyone's an Entrepreneur

IF YOU aren't entrepreneurial, you better learn to be.

I was lucky. I came to Hollywood with several businesses under my belt. Running a video-equipment rental outfit had taught me how to make money while working a job that was tangential to my long-term goals. Running a talent agency taught me how to walk away from a business that didn't align with my long-term goals, even if it was profitable. You don't have to have been a CEO to be a businessperson, though. You just need to recognize that succeeding in Hollywood requires more than talent—it requires business acumen.

The entertainment industry is just that: an *industry*. Like all industries, it is populated by businesses. As someone entering the industry, you need to start thinking of yourself as your own small business of one. If you're an actor, your talent is your product—but your business is developing and marketing that product. The same is true of producers, who launch a small business every time they start a new production. The industry's competitiveness and mercurial nature make virtually every job in Hollywood a position for a motivated entrepreneur, even if you get a W-2 instead of 1099s.

Your craft may have drawn you to the industry, but it is your business acumen that will allow you to succeed. Actors cannot only act, just as small-town doctors cannot solely diagnose and treat patients. Both have to learn to wear many hats. Doctors have to run their practices as businesses. They manage an office, oversee billing, hire and supervise staff, and do a million other administrative things. Hollywood is no different. Producers do far more than simply green-light projects. Running a production company requires hiring and supervising staff, drafting and maintaining budgets, answering phones and emails, maintaining relationships, and, yes, a million other administrative things.

Creatives face the same challenges. Beginning actors must do their own clerical and managerial work. They have to track payments, file tax forms, and maintain a budget that carries them between paychecks. Unless they are marketable names, they probably do their own PR, or at least work with a contract publicist.

Know Your Product

You really have to sell yourself in this industry—and in order to properly exploit your talent for profit, you are first going to have to figure out what your talent *is*. Find out what that thing is that you both like to do *and* are good at. Next, you're going to have to market that talent. That's the business side of the industry.

You should probably focus on one talent to start with. As I said earlier, abandon the multi-hyphenate approach to career building. Don't be a writer-director—be a writer or a director. Pick one role and prepare to work hard at it for years before you are taken seriously. If you want to be a cinematographer, learn the trade, and once you do, sell yourself at that trade. Then you can look to branch out into other areas. Doing so before you master a single marketable skill makes you look unprofessional.

No one is going to take you seriously if you introduce yourself as an actor-producer-writer-director who does sound and video editing on the side. Nothing draws a roll of the eyes from industry insiders faster than a business card claiming that you do everything in the industry. People go the multi-hyphenate route because they want to look useful and talented. But in the end, it just makes you look naive and unprofessional. Pursuing multiple disciplines before you master one smacks of amateurism. No one wants a jack-of-all-trades. They want to hire someone who is the best at the role they are hiring for.

You may be able to get away with being all of those things *if you have the track record to prove it*, but if you're new to the industry, you certainly don't have such a record. Few ever do. It's hard to master even one skill.

Have a Plan—Write It Down

Business School 101: Running a business requires a successful business plan. It is not enough to simply have a dream. And because you're going into the business of entertainment, you need to get into the habit of drafting detailed business plans. No matter what your discipline is, you need a plan that outlines the what, when, how, and why for each of your intended projects—as well as for your entire career. Sit down and outline your plans and put them down on paper. You can find sample business plans online if you need a model.

You need to draft plans for both long-term goals and short-term projects. All too often I see new filmmakers jump into a production without a real plan in place. In this digital age of inexpensive recording and editing equipment, anyone can wake up one day and decide to shoot a movie—but that doesn't mean they're ready to do so. Back when movies were shot on actual film, shooting was expensive. Now anyone can shoot hours of video at no cost, at least for the digital storage space, so you have filmmakers who start shooting before they are ready. Fewer and fewer new filmmakers actually plan ahead before they start shooting. Fewer still stop to think about *why* they are even doing what they are doing.

This off-the-cuff strategy does not result in "raw" filmmaking; it results in unfocused filmmaking. You need to understand why you are making the choices you are making as a filmmaker. Even the new crop of "mumblecore" directors, known for their highly improvisational style of filmmaking, have a plan for their films before they start—there is a why to their aimlessness.

Do research before you begin shooting. Understand what you are creating, as well as the context in which you are filming. If you are making a martial-arts film set in Japan, you need to know the history of the martial-arts genre and the current happenings as well. You want to observe and absorb content before you engage in creating your own so that you aren't doing damage control on your project later, trying to pull together loose ends and correct obvious mistakes. Know your vision at the outset.

Do not neglect long-term goals either. You need a master plan to keep you from going off track. People trying to make it in the industry flock to Hollywood each year, as they should.

Caught up in whirl of excitement, they pack their bags and show up in Los Angeles without a financial or business plan in place and end up taking a restaurant or office job to pay the bills.

There's nothing wrong with working a day job while you start your career, but you should have a plan in place to keep you from getting off track. If you have to take a restaurant job to pay rent, fine, but have a plan for applying to internships and breaking into the industry while working in the restaurant on nights and weekends. There are cheaper places than Los Angeles to just wait tables!

Whatever your plan, just make sure you have one—it will increase your chances of making it.

Businesses Have Budgets

No matter the size of your project, it needs a budget. Even the simplest, five-minute production must have a budget and a production schedule. Films are complex collaborations, and every step of a project must be planned ahead of time—and that means knowing what you can spend on what. You don't want to run out of money mid-project, nor do you want to finish a project and realize you could have afforded to spend more to make a better product!

You also need to keep a personal budget. If you're just launching your career, it is a good idea to keep your business costs low. One way to do this is to take a DIY approach, and handle as much of your business by yourself as possible. Learn to do your own makeup and hair. You don't need a dedicated manager or publicist right away, as you can usually do these things yourself.

Do realize, though, that it will eventually be important to

make such investments as your career progresses. But right now, you can't spend money you don't have, and racking up a mountain of credit card debt isn't going to help you reach your career goals.

Businesses Have Customers

You are a business, and your business has both customers and potential customers. Be able to identify them. No matter your discipline, realize that you are creating your own cottage industry, and figure out your customer base. If you're an actor, your customers include casting directors, agents, studio managers, producers, and more. Even your headshot photographer is a stakeholder in your business. Everyone who helps push you down the path to success is your customer and a stakeholder in your career. Treat them as such.

Recognize that your relationship with customers is a two-way street. You need them as much as they need you. They are paying (or potentially paying) you to do a job. The customer may not be right, as the adage claims, but you need to keep them happy regardless. You have to uphold your end of the bargain. That's just part of being a professional.

Treat your customers right. Be humble. No one likes a diva, and you will lose customers by acting like one. Be positive and professional with every person you encounter in the industry. Show them respect, and they're likely to do the same for you. Pretty much anyone you meet in the industry might be able to further your career, so you want to work hard to build a circle of industry people around you. These people—your customers—are instrumental to your success. They are going to help you achieve your career goals, but only if you keep them happy and help them fulfill their own goals and needs.

Building a customer base requires giving the right people access—by which I mean access to you. Building a Hollywood career is all about gaining access and fostering the right relationships. You want to make customers of the right people, many of whom simply won't have you on their radar unless you put yourself out there. Industry professionals aren't going to seek you out; you have to seek them out.

When it comes to selling yourself, follow the mantra popularized in *Glengarry Glen Ross*: Always be closing. People come to Hollywood to market themselves and everyone understands this, so don't feel bad for putting yourself out there. You have to be proactive to get noticed. If you are an actor, sell yourself as the right person for the roles you want. If you are a writer, don't be afraid to ask for pitch meetings. Producers are paid to take pitches. As long as you aren't rude or gauche, this shouldn't be a problem.

Treat People As You Want to Be Treated—Professionally

Follow up on everything. This is just plain courtesy and common business protocol. Get back in touch with people when you say you are going to, send thank-you notes when appropriate, and always respond to people, even if it is just to politely decline something. People might be disappointed if you turn down their offer or request, but they are likely to respect you for your decision if you respond in a professional manner.

Showing people this courtesy can pay off in the long run. A project or role that isn't appealing now might become appealing later in your career. Maybe you will hit a dry spell and a part that once seemed beneath you might now be a path back into the industry.

Even when you are starting out in the industry, you don't have to take every opportunity that comes your way, though many people do. Just be sure to entertain all offers respectfully and to be professional if you do have to turn something down. Sometimes a project is just not right for a certain stage of your career. That's fine. But treat people with respect and always follow up. Anyone who has taken an interest in you is a potential customer, even if they're not a current customer.

Of course, just because you play nice doesn't always mean others will. You should retain your composure even when others do not. Inevitably, people are going to slight you in the course of your career. If someone treats you unprofessionally or unkindly, don't hold a grudge or seek revenge. If their actions are egregious, you can sever business relations if necessary, but do it out of practicality, not out of spite. Revenge is never a good reason for action or reaction.

That said, be prepared to hold your ground. Sometimes other people will try to force you into uncomfortable, awkward, and even professionally dangerous situations. Heed your instincts in any situation that makes you uncomfortable, but be as diplomatic and practical as possible in your approach.

Don't Be Afraid to Market Yourself

Starting out, you will probably need to serve as your own publicist, so learn how to promote yourself. Don't be afraid to get out there. As I've said, people come to Hollywood in order to get noticed, so don't be hesitant to sell yourself—just don't be rude, overbearing, or needy.

No one knows who you are at this stage in your career, so it is up to you to get yourself out there. It's not enough to just show up at auditions. You need to actively promote yourself. Set aside time in your schedule to do this every week. Don't worry about not having a ton of money for marketing. There are lots of things you can do on a budget. Many restaurants and coffee shops will let you leave business cards and headshots in their foyers. Tack your résumé up on the corkboards at community and cultural centers. Attend networking meetings. Make sure that you leave a way for people to get in touch with you.

By marketing yourself, you are beginning to develop a brand that will take you to the next level. This will lay the groundwork of your career, so that when you do land an agent, hire a publicist, and take on a manager, those people will already have a core brand on which to build. But the truth is, most people have to be very actively engaged in self-promotion to ever get to that level.

Marketing is more than scattering headshots around town haphazardly. You want to create a consistent aesthetic and brand. Think about how aesthetic plays into brand development. Walk down the cereal aisle in a grocery store, imagining it as a red carpet. There are all of these different cereal brands with all kinds of packaging. What causes people to pick one sugary cereal over another? What makes Tony the Tiger and Count Chocula the superstars of the aisle, while other brands remain on the cereal D-list? The difference is marketing and promotion.

When building your own brand, make sure all of the pieces fit together. You want both consistency and cohesion. How you style your hair, what clothes you wear, how you do your makeup—these things matter. They coalesce into an overall personal brand. The entertainment industry is very image-oriented, especially if you're an actor or performer. But even if you're behind the camera, there's a very specific way people act and dress in Hollywood. You need to have the right image to succeed. Like it or not, this is important to launching your career.

Branding is something that you will have to work on for the entirety of your career, so get used to it now. Successful businesses are always moving forward, developing new products and tweaking their brand. You should always be doing the same with your personal brand. The entertainment industry is replete with tales of stars who burned out, washed up, or otherwise faded from relevancy. This does not have to be your fate. You don't have to become stale. Often what really happens is that these people, despite obvious talent, fail to adjust their brand to changing times. They fail to pivot right in their careers when circumstances change.

Everyone makes career missteps sometimes. The important thing is that you know how to get yourself back on track. Be mindful of changing circumstances and where your career is heading.

Pay Access Forward

Later on in your own career, once you are successful, newcomers to the industry will start seeking you out. Now it is your turn to give access to others. I always encourage people to share their knowledge, connections, and advice. Don't be stingy, and don't shut people out. You got to the top through the access and help other people gave you—now it's your turn to return the favor.

When I attend film festivals, I am always accosted by needy and sometimes even pushy people. Like most humans beings, I don't enjoy being approached so aggressively, but I try not to shut even these people out. I understand that as tactless as they might appear, these people are just like anybody else trying to make it in the industry. Others helped me get to where I am, and it would be wrong to pull the ladder up behind me.

I encourage you to do the same. Pay it forward. Give access to others, no matter where you are in your career path. This philosophy is what drove me to write this book and to found Your Hollywood Pro.

7

Can You Get Along with Others? Why Collaboration Is the Key to Success

IF CONTENT is king in Hollywood, then the golden rule of Hollywood is this: Collaboration is essential.

Hollywood is populated with creatives, on both ends of the camera. The industry is full of smart, talented people with good ideas—maybe great ideas. Even boring old industry suits like myself have creative ideas worth paying attention to sometimes! It is important to collaborate with others—it is, in fact, required. Making movies is not like writing poems. Emily Dickinson might have done great with nothing but a pen and solitude, but if she were going to make it in the entertainment industry, she'd have to learn to step out of the bedroom and into the boardroom, or theater hall, or film set, or writers' meeting. She would have to learn to collaborate.

Good ideas are essential, but they are nothing until they are executed. That script you wrote isn't worth much in the real world until a producer green-lights and bankrolls it, a director directs it, actors bring it to life, set designers give it a setting, and a team of crew members and others produce and distribute it. Good ideas that aren't brought to fruition might as well not exist—and bringing an idea to fruition requires collaboration.

There is a myth in the creative world that collaboration means compromising one's art. This causes self-proclaimed auteurs and know-it-all actors to cling to their original artistic vision at the cost of the improvement that collaboration confers. These people consider making a production that appeals to industry suits, and even an actual audience, a corruption of their artistic integrity.

This way of thinking won't get you very far in Hollywood, and it is not likely to get your project off the ground. No one wants to work for someone who is hard to work with.

Such an attitude is bad for your career, and it's bad for your art, too. Collaboration allows great minds to come together on a team. The result is very often greater than the sum of the parts. Of course, you don't have to take every last suggestion someone gives you on every project, even if they are studio suits. In my experience, though, Hollywood newcomers are more likely to be stubborn and egotistical than overly impressionable.

Dispel the myth of the writer alone at their desk. Writers for film and TV work in pairs or teams. And every project has multiple producers. Actually, there are so many producers on a project that, a few years ago, the Academy of Arts and Sciences set a limit of three producers per title in the Oscars; prior to that the dozens of producers would win an Oscar if the film won. It was a mess.

Of the many productions I have worked on to date, I have never worked with fewer than three other producers. Once I worked with fourteen. That's more people than there are on a courtroom jury! Getting this many people to come to a consensus on anything is difficult—and it becomes more so when you are dealing with so many artistic opinions.

So how do you do it? It is a very careful process. You start by looking for common ground. Rather than thinking about how you would do things differently, find the key points you agree on and start building consensus there. This approach can really keep a project moving forward despite competing opinions.

Above all, you must learn to listen to and cooperate with other talented people and other artists, many of whom might consider themselves your equals (and rightfully so). Collaboration allows for many people to pool their creative resources and make a good idea great. Think of it as an idea accelerator. Chances are, you're not always the smartest person in the room. And even if you are, I can assure you that you are rarely smarter than the combined total of everyone in the room. And there's nothing wrong with that. You are in an industry with thousands of other bright, creative people—so start collaborating with them!

Finding Collaborators

For those already in the entertainment industry, collaboration is just part of the job description. But for those still trying to break in, collaboration can be a tool for hammering out the kinks in your work. Seek out collaborators who can give you honest feedback. Friends and family can be an excellent group for a first-round peer review. The people who love you may be inclined to flatter you, but most will be honest if you ask them to. If you want to go a step further, put your idea in front of a room full of peers. If you are a writer, show your script to other writers. If you are an actor, rehearse your monologue or dialogue in front of other actors. Professional peers are aspiring A-listers just like you, and they'll tell you what they really think.

If you have the money and time to go to film school, this can be another resource for finding good readers. If not, don't worry about it. (As Quentin Tarantino once said, "When people ask me if I went to film school, I tell them, 'No, I went to films.'") Join a writing group. Move to Los Angeles and seek out like-minded professionals at industry parties and events. There are collaborators out there, you just have to find them.

Learn to Take Constructive Criticism Constructively

One thing to keep in mind: When you do solicit feedback, take it seriously and graciously—you asked for it. Act like a jerk, and no one is likely to give you feedback twice.

Feedback is part of the creative process. I recently sat on a film festival panel about the creative development process with a fellow producer. He complained that studio suits, as he called them, were always writing notes on his projects and telling him what to do. "That's their job!" I responded. "They have to give you notes on a project. It's what they're literally paid to do."

These suits are also the same people paying producers, writers, directors, actors, and everyone else in the industry—and I can assure you that we are not paying you to ignore our advice and feedback! Receiving and incorporating feedback is part of the development process. It is the process by which people in the industry collaborate. It may seem like forced collaboration at times—and sometimes it is—but it produces results. Collaboration helps refine and streamline creative projects.

Just because you started a project doesn't mean that you have all the answers. Collaboration means a willingness not to have to be 100 percent right, 100 percent of the time. It means realizing that other people have good ideas, too—recognize this fundamental truth, and you should have no problem taking criticism constructively.

You will be receiving feedback and criticism throughout your career, which means that you need to know how to not only roll with the punches but learn from the punches. I once asked a friend whose studio had rejected my script to pull my script coverage. Coverage refers to all of the notes and annotations that an agency or studio makes when reviewing a potential project. You need courage and a thick skin to read your own script with the coverage on top—most of the time it is quite harsh and negative. Typically, studios and agencies don't release coverage, because it can create an awkward situation for writers to see their work reviewed and dissected in this way.

But in this case, I had a friend at the agency willing to pull the coverage for me. I pored over it with trepidation. It read something like a mini-review from a movie critic, only it was many critics, and they actually worked in the industry. Yes, much of it was harsh. But I actually agreed with a lot of the criticism. I was able to glean what was wrong with my script and find room for improvement. When I went back and incorporated some of these critiques into the script, the result was a better script.

I didn't even know these readers with whom I was "collaborating" on my script. But I kept an open mind and "listened" intently to their comments. Did I change my script in answer to every suggestion? Of course not. But I considered the feedback carefully and incorporated the changes that I thought would improve the script.

Now this is a rather bizarre and unlikely form of collaboration.

Maybe you don't have access to studio coverage of your script. But similar collaborative efforts happen all of the time in brainstorming sessions, workshops, and classrooms, and in the private residences of hopeful screenwriters who exchange scripts.

Your Vision Counts, Too

When we think of collaboration, we often think of listening to and accepting the ideas of others—but this is only half of being a good collaborator. The other half of the equation is learning to effectively articulate your vision to others. You must be able to communicate your vision, plan, and preferences to everyone working on your project. This doesn't mean that you need to be dictatorial, but rather that you should make sure everyone knows exactly what you want from them. They should understand your vision.

Of course, articulating your vision and plan to others requires that you fully understand it yourself. This is why having a business plan is so important—it provides you with clarity so you can provide clarity to others. If you haven't articulated your vision on paper, you will struggle to share it effectively.

No matter how clearly you communicate your vision, you can be sure that every person working on a project—actors, directors, camera operators, lighting and set designers, and the studio producers funding the project—will have their own interpretation of your vision. Listening to their ideas will be a key part of your process.

But before you respond to someone else's idea, make sure you fully understand what they are saying. Nothing is worse than blasting someone for an opinion they didn't even hold. If you don't get what they're trying to convey, ask them to elaborate or restate. Don't be afraid to ask your colleagues questions. This holds especially true if their role is subordinate to yours, as they might not feel confident enough to speak up.

Creative people like to be listened to, and everyone wants to be taken seriously. You don't have to take all of their input, but you should consider it and know where they are coming from.

The Consummate Diplomat

To make it in Hollywood, you need to be diplomatic and congenial, and you need to be able to build relationships and work well with others.

Learn how to get along with everyone in the business, from creatives to suits, to crew. Hollywood is a people business, which means you won't do yourself any favors if you go around offending people. Find ways to compliment others, but more importantly, make sure you're listening to and understanding their point of view.

Take a deep breath before you respond to a colleague's critique, especially if you're doing it in person. Think before you speak, lest you say something you regret. You want to provide others the same honest and respectful critique that you want from them.

Don't be overly critical of other people's ideas. Remember, brainstorming and critique is where ideas come to fruition—they don't come to the meeting full-fledged. When I started working as an associate producer on my first TV show, I was amazed to see that 90 percent of what came out of the writers' room was total junk. But what I realized was that this had nothing to do with a lack of talent. This is just part of the writing process. Writers spend hours sitting around a table throwing out ideas, most of which are just awful. The writers find good material by trying lots of things and checking to see what resonates with others, what makes them laugh, what works. So don't blast someone for throwing out an idea that ultimately won't make it into the production anyway. Just politely suggest an alternative. It's all part of the process.

The truth is that collaboration on a large scale is slow, difficult, and messy. It can take hours to get a writing team to come together on a single piece of work. But what makes the cut in the end has been vetted and is generally of higher quality than what someone might have written on their own. That's another benefit of collaboration: It takes the onus off of any one person's shoulders. The work is divided up, and the good ideas can come from anyone.

Learn to Delegate

You can't go it alone in Hollywood, so in addition to learning to collaborate, you're also going to have to learn to delegate—yet another reason to avoid the lure of multi-hyphenation. Trying to be a writer, director, producer, and editor when you are really best at writing deprives you of the chance to match your genius writing with the best directors and producers at your disposal. You cannot produce your best work this way—no one does.

Consider Woody Allen, perhaps the most famous of the multi-hyphenate auteurs. He is notorious for running a production like a dictatorship—doing everything himself and retaining total artistic control of everything on the set. His method flies totally in the face of the Hollywood studio system. And yet, even Woody Allen defers to others. Actors who work with him regularly report that he allows them to interpret their role as they see fit. Woody Allen has certainly earned the right to control his productions, and he is known for doing so, but even he knows when to be collaborative and delegate authority.

Collaboration allows you to take the best ideas from the best sources and bring them together to make your project better. You aren't the master of everything. Delegate and defer to experts. Assume that the people around you on a studio set are just as talented as you are—how would they have gotten where they are otherwise?

Defer to those with more expertise. Nothing will hit the brakes on a project quite like insulting or ignoring the advice of someone in physical production. They are experts in the mechanics of making a movie and you need to respect their individual niches. Share your opinion with these colleagues, but be specific and constructive. Telling a lighting designer that he isn't exactly hitting your vision without giving good feedback doesn't really help him help you—it risks turning your project into a long, slow, expensive grind.

By delegating to those with the right expertise, you save yourself from having to worry about every last detail and you ensure that the best person for the job is on every job. Trust your colleagues. The average cable TV production has a minimum of one hundred people working on it. The average film production will have thousands. Micromanagement simply doesn't work when you are collaborating on this level. It will only anger your colleagues and slow down your project.

Just as you should avoid underestimating your peers and the industry suits, you should also be careful not to dismiss the newcomers. Early in my career, I was in a conference room with a dozen stand-up comedians, some of note, who were workshopping material for a new sitcom. They were too busy trying to best one another to listen to anything that the junior colleagues had to say. When I spoke up, they dismissed or belittled me. I kept my cool and let them have their way.

Ultimately, the sitcom was canceled after six episodes. This happens to most shows, and I'm not so pompous as to think that I had all of the right ideas either, but I do believe that if the more experienced writers would have listened to everyone there, we could have written better scripts collaboratively.

• • •

Differences of opinion on a project are common, but fights don't have to be. Failing to respect others will get you labeled as someone who is hard to work with—not an attractive hire or partner. You have to learn to accommodate other people's point of view, or you're never going to survive the production process, let alone the distribution and marketing that follows. If you don't learn how to collaborate early in your career, you may never have much of one to speak of. Luckily, collaboration is fun and highly productive—otherwise no one would do it.

8

Bringing It All Together—Your First Real Production

My FIRST major collaboration came long before I ever made it to Hollywood. This turned out to be advantageous, as I got to learn a lot about how Hollywood works and make some big mistakes early on, before I ever started working at a major studio. This was the time when a lot of the concepts I've introduced in this book really started to click for me. I began putting my skills into practice, drew upon my vast wealth of content knowledge, learned to hustle like an entrepreneur, and got a crash course in collaboration on a massive scale.

My first television production started out as a college project that, through sweat and perseverance, eventually became a real on-air TV show called *Lights Out*. I was only a freshman when we began working on the show. Our professors, most of whom were in their fifties and sixties and had decades of experience, were not initially supportive of a bunch of hot-shot students starting up a TV show. The head of our film department said we didn't know enough about the industry to produce a quality show. We certainly showed him!

Here's how it started: In 1988, as a college freshman at Texas Christian University in Fort Worth, I spotted a flier in the student union. "Want to be part of making a TV show? Give me a call," the flier read. In retrospect, it looked rather unprofessional, but I did want to be part of the making of a TV show. So I gave it a shot and dialed the number. The person who picked up on the other end was…another young college student with no real industry experience.

This was one of those times when taking a chance and learning to engage really paid off. Though I wouldn't have known it from our first phone conversation, the person I was speaking to would soon become a friend, a roommate, and my co-producer on a television show—as would another industry hopeful who'd answered the ad. The three of us had no experience producing a show, but we were willing to work late nights and long, unpaid hours to make it happen. And we were willing to work together—to learn to collaborate.

We planned to make a comedy variety show, like *The Tonight Show* or *Late Night*, and we started out by just goofing around, throwing out ideas, and filming on cameras we borrowed from my rental business. But we worked really hard on writing good scripts for the show.

Early on, we realized that we didn't have all of the tools, know-how, or skills necessary to really pull this off. We needed more collaborators, more people with different areas of expertise to delegate to and draw upon. We used the school as a resource and brought in people from the production department. The campus had an amazing production facility with two large soundstages, one big enough to shoot a TV show on. The film department, seeing that we were serious about our endeavor, allowed us to use the big stage to film our show.

So we started shooting. Our show was initially a spoof of *Late Night with David Letterman*, but we didn't have access to notable guests—so we had actors portray celebrities or knockoffs of celebrities. The college held screenings of the show, and we started filming in front of a live audience on the soundstage. We were getting great feedback.

We sent one episode we were particularly proud of to David Letterman, hoping he would invite our host, a Letterman spoof, onto his show. To put it mildly: Letterman was not interested. The NBC legal department fired back at us with a cease-and-desist letter. This shocked us at the time, but in retrospect, I consider it something of an honor. NBC and the show must have considered us something of a threat if they were bothering to demand that we stop. It was, in a way, a show of respect.

Did we stop there? No, we persevered. Threat of legal action gave us a chance to retool the show. We held a collaborative brainstorming session. This was your classic "write it all down" brainstorm. The department heads and producers met to throw out ideas and see what worked. There was a dry-erase board in the conference room the school had supplied us, and we spent hours writing down ideas, erasing them, making lists, finding common ground—and the ultimate result was the *Lights Out* format. It was less a spoof than a real comedy variety show composed of short skits—like *Saturday Night Live*, although admittedly more juvenile. We also planned to get real guests and to take the show to a bigger audience. Through collaboration, we turned what could have been a lawsuit into the opportunity to create a better product. We put pen to paper and started drafting new plans.

Our plans required even more collaborators, and also more of our time. We spent every moment not at class in our school-supplied conference room working on the show. We took on longer hours. We put in seven-day weeks. We worked harder than we ever had before. It was exhausting going to school at the same time, but this seemed like the best of all possible ways to pay one's dues.

As the production became increasingly complex, we took on specialized roles. We were beginning to look more like a real production by the day, even though everyone was working for free. We had someone in charge of marketing, someone in charge of writing, and someone in charge of finding and handling talent. Everything was delegated to the most appropriate person for the job. The latter role went to me because of my experience running a talent agency (never mind that it was only for exotic dancers!). In order to move away from being a spoof show, we had to get actual guests. I made hundreds of calls to publicists and agents in Hollywood, soliciting talent for the show. To my surprise, many said yes!

This experience taught me how to talk to industry suits comfortably. We set up meetings with local TV stations to try to find someone to put us on the air. We had the spoofy version of the show in the can to show as a product, the beginnings of a production crew, and a cease-and-desist letter that we were now quite proud of! We eventually landed an actual network deal with KTVT, a superstation based in the Dallas–Fort Worth area that broadcasted in thirty-eight states at the time. We couldn't believe it! *Lights Out* was going to be on the air, nearly nationwide.

The station had one stipulation, though: We were responsible for selling the advertising ourselves. No advertisers and sponsors, no deal.

We could have been deterred. We could have declined the offer and looked for another deal that may or may not have materialized. Instead, we seized upon the opportunity in front of us and commenced to learn the marketing side of the business, knowledge that has been invaluable in my work as a Hollywood executive. We were determined and willing to venture outside of our comfort zones. If we didn't know how to do something, we learned to—or we brought on someone with the right expertise. That's the kind of perseverance and resourcefulness it takes to really beat the odds.

In this case, we hired a sales manager from the business department at our college, who began cold-calling companies in the Dallas area, from mom-and-pop stores to *Fortune* 500 firms. Once we had sold enough thirty-second ads to appease the studio, we went back to the station. They seemed amazed that three college kids and their friends had been able to pull this off. They gave us a time slot, and we began production of the new-and-improved *Lights Out*.

Though we had just started, we refused to get stale. We were constantly hard at work on content and brand building, and it showed. Our product was getting ever better. The production values improved, we had stronger writers, and the show started attracting real guests. We interviewed George W. Bush, who was "only" the owner of the Texas Rangers baseball team at the time. Tony Dorsett, Dallas Cowboys legend, came on the show to announce his retirement from professional football, which got us local and national press.

So we had content. We were learning to collaborate. We were being entrepreneurial and pursuing the project both creatively and as a business. We were giving it our all and persevering.

Unfortunately, despite all of this, we weren't making enough money. Our ratings weren't bad, but they were low enough to jeopardize the show. The station could make more money running infomercials—and ultimately that's the route they took. This gave me a great appreciation for the financial realities of a large production. At the end of the day, it's not enough to create art—you have to create art that sells and you have to find a market for your work.

We had only filmed a half-dozen episodes at this point, and we still wanted to keep the show going. So we began talking with the local Fox affiliate—this was back when Fox was first emerging as a major broadcast network—and pitched them the show. One of the producers was amenable; he saw the marketing value in a show that could be billed as being produced completely by college kids.

Unfortunately, when *The Simpsons* and *Married with Children* came out and the Fox network blew up, this producer was replaced with a new head of programming who wasn't even interested in taking our meetings. He had zero interest in *Lights Out*, and we didn't have a B-pitch ready. Ironically, this was possibly our biggest mistake on *Lights Out*—not anything we'd done wrong with the production, but the fact that we didn't have a backup plan ready at a time when we could have leveraged the show's success in order to move in a different direction. If we had been better prepared with a B-pitch, we might have been able to use our first show to launch a new one—but we didn't. So that was the end of that.

In the wake of this major disappointment, as I discussed earlier, I fell into a state of deep self-doubt and considered leaving the industry for good. Luckily I didn't, and in retrospect, I realize that *Lights Out* introduced me to almost every aspect of the industry at a very young age. We learned so much about writing, producing, filming, marketing, distribution, and production. We had run an entire production ourselves, putting together the full specs, and placed a show on broadcast television. Not bad for a bunch of twenty-year-old kids! Sure, we had now run out of gas on the project, but we had learned and accomplished a lot, and my work with *Lights Out* positioned me for much of the success that would later follow.

But first I had to dust myself off, ditch that boring day job, and keep on keeping on. If you take only one thing away from this chapter, let it be that: The trick to making it is never to give up. You have to persevere.

PART III

Carry Your Script Wherever You Go? Give Me a Freaking Break!

9

Brush Up Your Social Skills: Making the Connections that Will Launch Your Career

HOLLYWOOD IS an industry built on forging relationships and connections. It is therefore a great tragedy and a great irony that so many creative people tend to be so introverted. Many find themselves simply exhausted by people (especially on the seventh day of a film festival). If you identify more as an introvert than an extrovert, I am sorry to tell you that you'll have to come out of your shell. Networking is all but required in Hollywood, so you will need to learn how to forge connections.

While it is probably true that some people are natural extroverts and others are simply not, it is also true that the traits of an extrovert can be practiced and learned. But, as with everything else, you are going to have to work at it. You need to identify the fear or the frustration that keeps you from wanting to go out and meet people. Once you figure out the cause of your anxiety, you need to find a way to manage it.

Focus on the advantages you do have. Being outgoing is easier when you have something in common with the people you are talking to. Luckily, you have at least one thing in common with virtually everyone in Hollywood: movies. That's your safe place, the thing you can fall back on and talk about for hours.

There is no greater compliment you can pay someone after a Q&A session or during a cocktail party than approaching them to ask about their role in creating their latest project. They won't find you creepy, and they won't think you're weird or insecure. They may even talk to you for longer than you wanted them to! People in the entertainment industry generally enjoy talking about their experience. You'll have successfully made a new contact and learned something in the process. That's worth getting out of the house for—and all you had to do was talk about movies!

You don't have to think of attending events as "being social." Going to a cocktail party or another industry function is part of your job. You are engaging and networking and learning. If it's your first or second event, you can absolutely just go and observe. When I interned with Mark Logan, he gave me tickets to a table ad sale convention in Dallas. He didn't want to go, so I went by myself. I didn't know anyone, and I didn't talk to anyone there. At work the next week, though, he asked if I'd gone, and I was able to say that, yes, I'd gone. It's that first step toward making connections, and for me, it was just scouting the scene. I didn't have any anxiety because I went in viewing the event as a low-pressure engagement.

If you are nervous about interacting, try to just go and learn the lay of the land at these events. The more time you spend at these kinds of events, the more comfortable with them you will become. And as you get more comfortable, you will get better at networking. Just being at events opens up opportunities to make connections.

Early on in my Hollywood career, I went to another event by myself. Because I was alone, I felt out of place and uncomfortable. I didn't talk to anyone at all. The next Monday I ran into someone at work who'd wanted to go to the event, and I was able to drop the line, "Oh, I went to that! What do you want to know?" He became a contact, which is a great reminder about sharing your access with other people as much as you can. The more events you attend, the more chances you have for interactions of all kinds.

At the very next event that I attended for Mark, I actually ended up talking to almost everyone there. I ran into a lot of media ad salespeople, and they asked where I was interning and if I'd gone to the convention in Dallas. I told them I'd definitely been there. Even though I hadn't done anything that first time except watch, I was able to say, "Yes, I was at the convention in Dallas." And because of this, they viewed me as an ambitious up-and-comer—someone who was part of the scene and industry. Everyone gave me their business cards without my having to ask for them, and that was a small victory. Just accumulating contacts and putting in face time are victories in and of themselves.

Fending Off the Perk Protectors

Offices have all kinds of personality types. One that is common to many workplaces is what I like to call "The Perk Protector." This is the person who hoards all of the invitations that get passed out. Don't let them hog the networking opportunities! If someone in your office is bent on attending every event, ask if you can be their guest. You might not want to go with them—especially if they're more interested in free food than networking opportunities—but you can break off from them later in the evening, and I suggest that you do.

If the Perk Protector won't give up or share their invites, just ask them why they're going. Tell them that you're hoping you can go because there's a specific person that you want to meet at that cocktail party, or that your girlfriend is an artist and wants to attend that exhibit. Give a solid reason for why you need to be there. If that person is just going to the event for the free food or giveaways, offer to bring them back something.

Whatever you do, don't let the Perk Protector hog all of the networking opportunities that are supposed to be available to everyone in the office.

How to Make that First Meeting Work for You

There is a right way and a wrong way to go about approaching people in Hollywood. Systems and etiquettes are in place for a reason; you deviate from them at your own peril. You want to approach potential customers in the right manner, through the right channels, with an appropriate attitude.

I was once on a panel about breaking into filmmaking. My fellow panelists were all actively involved in the entertainment business, mostly as producers. What some people don't know is that executives are not allowed to take unsolicited pitches. Pitches must come via established agents only. At the beginning of the panel, the moderator announced that attendees were not to pitch ideas to us. Nevertheless, a woman came up to me after the event and launched straight into a pitch.

She had made a documentary on a niche subject, and the

first thing she asked me was, "Can I send you my movie so you can take a look at it?" She'd leaped into step number 560 of networking before she even knew me—I don't think she even knew my name yet! She just saw that I was a Hollywood executive. Translation: another suit to toss her movie at in her carpet-bomb campaign for studio distribution.

I told her politely—and repeatedly—that I wasn't allowed to take outside pitches. She wouldn't listen, and I had to abruptly extract myself from the conversation. I thought that was the end of it. I was wrong. The next Monday, I received an email from her. (Note that Monday is not the best day to follow up with people, because they're swamped with whatever has accumulated over the weekend. You're more likely to get the attention you want on a Tuesday.)

I had given her my personal email address, since I had attended the conference as an individual, not on behalf of my studio. Nevertheless, she had gone online and looked up my work email and used that instead. That was strike one. Strike two was that she had copied both her manager and her lawyer on the email. The message contained a link to her movie and said, "Please let me know if this is something your company would be interested in."

Not only had she taken what personal connection we had and turned it into a solicitation move with my company, she had also put me in the awkward and legally perilous position of having received an unsolicited pitch. By doing so, she had moved from a gauche annoyance to a real threat, and I had to hand the case over to the legal department. (The studio doesn't want to be sued by someone who sent us an unsolicited pitch and now thinks that we "stole" their idea for a romantic comedy because our newest movie is both a romance and a comedy. This is why we have legal departments and why we don't take unsolicited pitches, by the way.)

This woman ruined any chance to work with our studio, now or in the future. She clearly chose the wrong way to go about introducing herself to me. First impressions count, and as they say, you only get one shot at them.

Again, there is a right way and a wrong way to approach people in Hollywood.

I was lucky enough to meet Oliver Stone at a casting call in Dallas back when I was working for the Kim Dawson Talent Agency. I was maybe twenty at the time. The director was casting *JFK*, which I consider to be one of his masterpieces, and there were thousands of people on hand. Only a hundred or so would end up in the movie, but they all showed up, ready to engage.

I saw Oliver Stone walking down the line of people. He appeared to be looking the crowd up and down, very likely to see if anyone stood out to him for parts or for extra work. He had an entire entourage with him: the casting director, the casting assistant, the casting assistant's assistant. As he approached, I casually stepped out of line. Since I was representing two women from the talent agency that day, I was wearing a suit instead of whatever normal college kids wore, and Stone made a crack about me being overdressed for an extras gig. I laughed, and I was polite, and I explained to him that I was there representing the agency, and he actually wound up casting one of the women.

As Stone proceeded down the line, a guy stepped out of the crowd and started yelling, "Mr. Stone! Mr. Stone!" He seemed out of it and not entirely stable, but Stone was very kind and respectful, and he went over to the man.

Then there was this awkward silence.

It turned out that the man had nothing to say once Stone got to him. The guy looked at this world-famous director standing in front of him, went silent, and handed Oliver Stone a banana.

Take care not to abuse or misuse a chance encounter. There were thousands of people waiting to interact with Stone that day. A few of us did. I got work for my talent. Another guy handed him some fruit. Which person do you want to be?

I had no idea that I was going to run into Stone that day, but when I did, I respected the proper boundaries. I treated him like a human being, I acted like a professional, and I got rewarded for it. It's all about your approach—your style, the way you carry yourself. If you have a relevant topic to discuss with someone, you can get even further.

As I progressed in the business, I started to understand that giving someone your script is generally an awkward, unsociable approach. It's asking a lot of someone to read your script—particularly someone you don't even know. If I'd used that audience with Oliver Stone to hand him my script, I probably would've been treated no differently than the guy who handed him the banana. Instead, I used those twenty seconds to pitch my client in a way that was appropriate to the time and place, and, in doing so, got her one step farther on the path to success.

Social Media Is No Silver Bullet

The way you hear people talk about social media today, you would think that it has completely revolutionized the world to the point where we are all little Facebook-Twitter-LinkedIn cyborgs, part man, part social media machine. The truth is that while social media is truly a great modern tool for kindling your connections, social media is not a one-stop shop for all of your networking needs. Social media won't replace the need to make face-to-face connections, especially in Hollywood. No one has ever launched a career, or even finished a project, by sitting behind their computer and posting to social media websites. Close professional connections are rarely made entirely on social media—I doubt anyone has ever sold a script with Facebook.

The caveat here, as you may have noticed, is that I qualified all of that by saying *entirely* or *only* with social media. People can and do further projects and careers by using social media. If you can use a well-done Kickstarter campaign to fund a short film that gets you into a festival where you meet an agent who hooks you up with a studio to produce a feature-length movie… well, good for you! Congratulations!

But congratulate yourself, not social media, because it was only one small step in that process. Social media is a tool, but it won't take you from beginning to end. Social media won't do the job for you. Making connections, finishing projects, and forging a career path can only be done by you and it is going to require face time and getting out of the house to attend events, gatherings, and (hopefully) your studio job or shoot.

If you do use social media, don't restrict yourself just to general social media tools, like Facebook and Twitter. Look into industry-specific social media websites, such as Stage 32 (www. stage32.com), which I use. That is a good way to meet people, but don't just go on there and add friends for no reason. Use it to help make real-world connections. Sites like Slated (www. slated.com) can help you forge higher-level connections in the industry, as well as financing and sales. My recently launched website, Your Hollywood Pro (www.YourHollywoodPro.com), is a good resource for meeting industry professionals who can give you custom-tailored career advice. There are many other great sites out there as well and more pop up all of the time.

But at the end of the day, just know you cannot rely solely on these websites to get you where you want to be. They are supplemental to face-to-face networking and actual industry work, not substitutes for them. If someone offers you a lifetime subscription to IMDb Pro, or you can afford it on your own, it can be great to have. I use it, and so should you. But you will almost always get farther by booking a ticket to a conference or event like American Film Market and hanging out in the hotel lobby or at seminars meeting producers, foreign financiers, and other industry professionals.

10

Surviving and Thriving at a Film Festival

MOST FILMMAKERS, actors, and producers attend a film festival at some point in their career. My advice is not to wait for that first invite to fall into your lap. Pursue these events now. Film festivals are great ways for aspiring actors, directors, and writers to meet industry players and other people with similar interests. Also, film festivals are great fun! Anyone in the industry can benefit from the experience, but festivals are especially important for filmmakers, particularly young ones. Getting a film into a festival could launch a filmmaker's career, and often does. Attend these festivals. Get your work into them if you can. Just get involved in as many ways as you can.

Some of the best-known festivals are Sundance, South by Southwest, and Cannes. If you get the opportunity to attend one of the big festivals, obviously you should go, but don't be afraid to check out smaller festivals, too. There are thousands of them out there, be they local, regional, or niche. Attending and taking part in any festival can be a great career move, so long as the festival is professionally run and you make the most of the opportunity.

If you live in or near a major city, there will be many high-quality local film festivals available to you. Attending a local festival can help you save on expenses, such as travel and accom-modations, as well as the higher registration fees of the major international festivals. Cannes is worth the investment if you get an invite, but those are in short supply and hotel rooms in the French Riviera don't come cheap. There's nothing wrong with launching your career at a festival close to home, and local festivals have the added benefit of allowing you to rally friends and family for support. This can be especially helpful if you are attending as a presenter—you want supportive people cheering you on and buoying your spirit. Participating in local festivals can be a stepping-stone to larger festivals.

If you're going to a festival that requires travel, check to see if the organizers can help with accommodations. If you have a film in the festival, this might be a possibility, even if it is not advertised. If you don't have a film in the festival, it's still worth checking out as the organizers might have connections in the city. Festivals often partner with hotels and offer attendees group rates that are substantially lower than the going price, especially in major metropolitan areas. Always ask politely for the best deals and rates that the film festival can get you. Be polite, but there's no need to be sheepish. Many successful people in the industry started out with limited means—they understand.

Where you sleep matters less than where you spend your waking hours, so you don't have to break the bank on a hotel room. Festivals are often hosted at major hotels or convention centers. The talent, media, and industry insiders will be housed at the main hotel, but those rooms can be expensive, even at the conference rate. Stay there if you can, but don't worry if you have to stay off-site for budgetary reasons. You shouldn't be spending that much time in your room anyway. These are networking events, which means you need to be out and about as much as possible.

Festival organizers book hotels in tiers, and there will usually be at least one relatively cheap hotel close enough to access on foot or by transit. Some festivals have volunteers who will shuttle you between the festival and off-site hotels, especially if you are an actor or a filmmaker participating in the festival.

Treat these volunteers kindly—and all the rest of them, too. At smaller festivals, the organizers may themselves be volunteers. Whether the people shuttling you back and forth are the festival's creative director or film school students, treat them with respect. Everyone deserves kindness and respect, especially the people working for free to make these amazing events happen. Also, you never know who these volunteers are—or who they will go on to be. Many aspire to work in the industry, and at least some of them will make it. Today's volunteer might become tomorrow's industry connection, so befriend them.

Volunteers can also be helpful in the here and now. They are often called upon to guard the doors of VIP areas, private parties, and celebrities' rooms, so they can be key in gaining access to events and people. Don't try to manipulate your way into an event or con your way into an audience with a celebrity—that's just bad manners—but do play nice with volunteers. They might be able to introduce you to someone or get you on the list for a private event.

Play Nice with the Other...Everybody

Be sure to give the same respect to other people at the festival, too. Treat the festival's organizers and staff, as well as the staff of the associated hotels and venues, as if you owe them something, because, in a lot of ways, you do. The festival organizers picked your movie, or picked you through an association with the movie, to be a part of the festival. You are very much in their debt. Reciprocate the favor if and when you can, however you can. The least you can do is to be polite, grateful, and kind.

Don't make them regret extending their invitation to you. Behave professionally and tactfully at all times. If you show up at a festival acting like a prima donna, the festival organizers are not likely to invite you down the red carpet again.

Getting on their good side of the festival organizers, though, can pay dividends. They can help you stand out from the crowd—which, depending on the festival's size, could feature hundreds or even thousands of people trying to do the same things you are. You may be just one of a hundred-plus filmmakers with a movie at the festival. While it is a thrill to be around so many people who share your interests and pursuits, it can make getting noticed difficult.

There are all kinds of ways that the management can help you with PR and marketing at the festival. They can get you better time slots for your screening and any talks. Primo spots go to the biggest celebrities, of course, but you don't have to have the best slot to nab a better slot. Making friends with the festival organizers may not get you a slot with the headliners, but it may keep your film from being screened at eight in the morning on the opening Thursday of a weekend festival.

Festival organizers can also help with publicity. With so many titles screening, the festival cannot possibly feature all of the films in the festival in national press or even local press. Still, almost every festival will have a dedicated publicist or press agent, and you should try to meet this person. Making nice with management and the PR professionals ups your chances of getting noticed via better publicity and higher visibility at the festival.

Play nice with the other filmmakers, too. Just because they are your competition doesn't mean you should be anything less than civil and collegial. Don't be pompous or rude around your peers. You want to create allies, not enemies. Your competition today is very likely to be a collaborator tomorrow. They might be someone working on your next project. They might ultimately be the person who hires you—or chooses not to hire you—for your next job.

The entertainment business is a small community. There are much fewer than six degrees of separation between most people in the industry. In my experience, everyone in the industry knows at least one person in common, so news and gossip travel fast and linger.

I once attended a festival where a new documentary filmmaker showed up acting like a diva. She disrespected the other filmmakers and the hotel staff and was constantly making demands of the festival organizers. By the end of the week, everyone at the festival knew her not for her work but for her notorious behavior. This was nearly ten years ago, and to this day, she hasn't broken free from the festival circuit. She was an A-lister at that festival, but she's never really made it big. There's no way to know for sure, but it's reasonable to assume that her attitude is at least contributing to holding her back.

Don't discount the importance of chance meetings with the food or beverage sponsors at events either. They are there to build their brands, and they like meeting people in the industry. Connections like these can lead to jobs, sponsorships, or gigs down the road. Everyone needs content these days, and nothing will get you noticed faster than a catchy viral video. These are often created and publicized by private companies.

The bottom line is this: Always be pleasant and treat everyone with respect.

Be mindful of your attitude at all times. Jerks aren't likely to stop being jerks, no matter what I tell them. But you don't actually have to be a jerk to act like one. Festivals can be very exciting, and they bring out the diva in some people. Don't be one of those people—it is neither becoming nor conducive to networking.

If You're an Actor (or Filmmaker), Act the Part

There is more to film festival etiquette than just playing nice. If you're part of the industry, or aspiring to be, now is the time to start acting like it. You want to exude the sense that you belong. This doesn't mean being pompous or pretentious. It means being professional. Comport yourself as the organizers, talent, and filmmakers do—not as the layperson attendees and audience members do. It's also generally best in the industry, as in life, not to come off as a stalker.

Don't ask celebrities for autographs. Professionals don't want other professionals' autographs—they want their acquaintance.

People are always bringing celebrity merchandise and memorabilia to film festivals to get it autographed. This behavior will make you look unprofessional at best, and stalker-crazy at worst. On the other hand, treating celebrities like the real people they are can put them at ease, making it possible to forge connections with them.

Anyone who works in Hollywood is familiar with how quickly a celebrity sighting can turn into a scene. Once, I was at the premiere of *Broadway: The Golden Age* at the Sunset Five Theater in Los Angeles. Naomi Watts, who wasn't even part of the project, was there to attend the Q&A as an audience member. She was spotted going into the venue, and by the time the movie was over, a group of celebrity hounds had gathered at the barricade to accost her on her way out. They had posters, headshots, and other memorabilia they wanted autographed. Some even had Naomi Watts action figures! I don't know what kind of person carries this stuff around with them in the off chance that they'll run into their favorite star, but word of advice: If you are the kind of person who carries a Naomi Watts action figure in your back pocket, you're not someone Naomi Watts wants to meet.

Seeing all of this happen, I went over and politely introduced myself. Not being part of the production, she didn't have any representation, handlers, or security there and was visibly uncomfortable. I offered to escort her to the parking garage, and we chatted a bit on the way there. She thanked me profusely before driving off. The lesson here is not to turn a chance encounter with a celebrity into something that is going to make you look crazy, desperate, or clueless. Treat celebrities like people and offer to be helpful, and you just might make a celebrity contact.

You might even make a friend. My sister and I once attended an after-party for a new movie that put a hot young actor on the map. Watching the talent come down the red carpet, I noticed that one of the actors had come without a publicist, so he didn't have anyone there helping him. My sister and I volunteered to be his make-do handlers. We escorted him down the red carpet, walked him around the event, and hung out with him and his girlfriend after the movie, staying out way too late and drinking way too much—in other words, we had a blast. He's actually still a good friend today, and while we haven't yet collaborated on anything professionally, we keep in touch.

In both of these cases, I was able to make industry connections simply by treating celebrities like real people and offering to help them out in a pinch. I wasn't creepy, clingy, pushy, or anything else. I was around, I was nice, and I treated them like I would anyone else whom I wanted to get to know.

If you want to be taken seriously in this business, don't be a photo bomber. Nothing reveals you as part of the crowd faster than asking talent to do a photo shoot with you. It's very unprofessional. Don't snap pictures of celebrities either, unless your Hollywood dream is being part of the paparazzi.

Don't worry if a photographer, or even just a friend, happens to snap a shot of you engaged in legitimate conversation with the talent. A candid image of you engaging at the event, casually taken by someone else, is fine. This is a far cry from tapping a celebrity you have never met on the shoulder and asking them to be a part of your selfie as you stand there smiling with your arm around them. You can't really be a celebrity hound and a

Hollywood professional at the same time. So leave your camera at home with your Naomi Watts action figures.

A lot of people get the urge to do these things when they aren't used to being around celebrities or famous filmmakers. Take my advice and learn from the mistakes of others. You should be acting like a professional, even if you haven't broken into the industry just yet. This isn't even really a case of "Fake it till you make it." It's more like, "Be it if you hope to ever become it." The choice to comport yourself as a professional is just that, a choice, and one you can make now.

Do All the Things

When attending a festival, stay in the immediate vicinity of the festival. Attend everything you can. You should be going to literally every party, every event, every sponsored meal, every Q&A—everything, period. Let the film festival be your full-time job while you're there. Most festivals don't last more than ten days, and the local ones are usually much shorter. Take the week or a long weekend off from work, and go to as many events as humanly possible.

Life being what it is, though, taking off a whole week to attend a festival isn't always feasible. Even if you can stay for the entire festival, events usually run concurrently, so you are going to have to prioritize and strategize in order to get the most out of your time. Cluster your schedule around the festival's biggest events. Check the festival directory and website to find out what the highlights are—such as a screening by a major filmmaker or a talk with a major celebrity—and attend these. The opening and closing screenings tend to be hallmark events, so try to attend these, too.

Whatever you do, stay at the festival! Festivals are often held in resort towns or cosmopolitan cities where there are a million other things to do. Don't do them. Don't go on any personal adventure. You came here to network and research, not sightsee. Take your meals at or near the festival as well. There will often be luncheons and events, many with free food and drinks. Eat there if possible, or at nearby restaurants where other festivalgoers tend to gather. Your goal is to maximize your opportunity to meet people in the industry.

Early in my career, I volunteered at a film festival event before the screening. I got to stay and watch the show and attend the Q&A. Afterward, I overheard that a small group of the filmmakers and actors, including Shelley Duvall, were headed to a local bar for drinks. I showed up and sat down at the bar. They recognized me as a volunteer, as I had previously introduced myself, and I wound up next to Shelley Duvall, who is probably best known for her role in *The Shining*. We talked a lot about her new film and the industry. She was an absolute delight and very insightful. She revealed aspects of her role that hadn't occurred to me while watching the movie, instantly making me want to rewatch the film and keep an eye out for the performance techniques she'd described to me. I learned a lot about filmmaking. I also learned how to better handle myself around celebrities.

This exchange was not due to luck, not totally. I made myself available by participating in the festival, and I wasn't afraid to talk to a celebrity when I had the chance.

A common mistake at festivals is to just go to screenings and watch movies. If you are shy, worn-out, or uncertain, you may be tempted to hide in darkened theaters all day. Resist this urge. Screenings are a major part of the festival, of course, but don't sacrifice face time with industry people to sit in the dark and watch a movie you can catch later at your local theater.

This is a rookie mistake, but industry veterans can make it, too. I have a friend and colleague who loves attending film festivals, but all he does is go to screenings. The festival is not a glorified theater. Good luck finding famous actors and up-and-coming filmmakers who are giving Q&As at your local AMC the following week! My friend is not taking advantage of the unique things that festivals have to offer. You should be focusing on events rather than screenings. You are looking for networking opportunities where you can interact with industry people.

11

How to Make the Most Out of a Q&A: They Have Questions...You Better Have Answers

Q&As ARE very common events at film festivals. They're great for learning about the industry, which is of course their intended purpose, but they are also wonderful platforms for networking in that they provide front-row seats to the industry. Q&As are a venue in which you get face-to-face access to industry insiders ready to field your questions. That's amazing and invaluable.

Q&As often take place after screenings at film festivals, and if you are going to take two hours to watch the movie, you should definitely take fifteen minutes to hang out afterward for the talk. But film festivals aren't the only places to find good Q&As—they take place just about everywhere in the entertainment world. They're used as promotional or marketing tools for films, and many theaters will host Q&A sessions on opening nights as part of an awareness campaign. They also happen at conventions and other industry events. So if you live in a big city, or even a moderately sized one, you're likely to find some in your area.

Make sure that you're on the online mailing lists of your local film festivals and film groups so that you can find out about these opportunities before they're common knowledge, as good Q&As sell out very fast. You can sometimes get free promotional tickets through alternative weeklies, local radio stations, and social media, so be sure to check these regularly. Check the websites of nearby theaters, too, as they will often host these as part of a film's release. When it comes to film festivals, know that the popular Q&As may have limited seats. You'll have to act quickly or pull some strings to get an invite—that's one reason being nice to festival organizers is so important!

Once you have your Q&A tickets in hand, it's time to do some planning. Arrange to take someone with you if possible. Having a date or a friend for moral support can give you the courage to hang around after the event without feeling awkward. These events often run late and over, so don't bring someone who can't sit still and look engaged. It's best to take someone who's genuinely interested in the event, but as long as your companion respects and understands that you are doing professional networking and research, they will be an asset.

Arrive early. There is likely to be a line and you want to be sure you get in and get a good seat, up front if possible. Use the time you spend in line to meet the people around you. Some are there just to see their favorite celebrity, but many will have the same genuine interest in partaking in the Q&A experience as you do. The latter are the folks you want to connect with and sit next to once you get inside. You don't want to be sitting next to someone who ends up asking silly, ridiculous, or even rude questions of the talent—you may be wrongly associated with them. Guilt by association will kill your chances of meeting the talent after the Q&A, especially if this person hangs around you. This is why attending with a like-minded professional can be a good thing—but if you must go alone, choose your seatmates wisely.

Pay attention during the film so that you can ask intelligent questions during the Q&A. Take notes if you have to. Scribbling thoughtfully in a moleskin may sound like nerd-alert material, but I promise you that no one notices and that the smart people are doing this, too. People take notes all the time at these events, and they are recognized as professionals or aspiring professionals. Their attention is appreciated.

Not asking a question at a Q&A is a missed opportunity. But asking a bad question is even worse! So watch carefully, take notes, and prepare a thoughtful question to ask afterward that will show how engaged you are. Q&As typically take a few minutes to get started. So use that time to craft a question that really knocks it out of the park. Don't ask something pretentious or convoluted. This is a Q&A, not your film school thesis defense. Ask an insightful and succinct question about the film or the filmmaking process. This question will be your first direct contact with the talent, and if it is not a good one, it will likely be your last. Make sure your question is about the movie that just screened, not the talent's back catalog. Asking a long-time director about a favorite movie is risky. It may not be *their* favorite. Or they might be tired of talking about it. That can put you in an awkward position with the filmmaker, leading them to brush you off.

It never hurts to be the first person to ask a question at a Q&A. In fact, it shows enthusiasm. Audience members are often shy or afraid to go first—don't be one of them. Have your super-smart question ready to fire off once the credits roll and the lights come on, but don't appear overeager. Just calmly raise your hand. If you get called on first, you'll certainly be noticed by whoever is taking questions, as well as the rest of the people in the room.

You asked a question—now listen to the answer. This may seem obvious, but in the excitement of firing off your question and being around major talent, you might forget to actually listen to the answer. Listen carefully so you can ask an appropriate follow-up question, either then or later if you're able to catch the talent after the Q&A.

Do not get up and leave before the Q&A is over—or any point during the event, for that matter. It might offend the talent or make studio executives nervous about the movie's prospects. Stay seated and wait for everything to come together. This is the portion of the event you should be coming for in the first place!

If someone in the front row does walk out before the event is over, feel free to take their seat. Doing so can be a sign of respect. I saw this happen at a Q&A session with Noah Baumbach, the director of *Frances Ha* and *The Squid and the Whale*. This was the beginning of his career, before he was as famous as he is now, and he looked very uncomfortable until a few people moved up to take the prime seats. This cleared the air and allowed Baumbach to crack a joke about the situation. He gave the people who changed seats the chance to speak next, and they were sort of in on the joke.

Resist the urge to bring your script or pitch to a Q&A. It's neither the time nor the place. I have seen this happen a dozen times at Q&As. Someone raises their hand, and the filmmaker calls on them, but rather than asking a question relevant to the movie everyone in the room just watched, the person launches into a thinly veiled pitch of their script. When it comes to Q&As, this is the faux pas to end all faux pas.

Sometimes people do this because they lack basic understanding of social skills, but more often than not, it is an act of desperation. They think it is their one opportunity to sell their idea. It's not. Spoiler alert: The filmmaker is not going to nod his head and say, "Great idea! Sold. Q&A canceled. Come with me, dear friend, we're going to make a movie!" Development executives don't hang out at Q&As hoping someone makes an interesting pitch in the form of a question. I have never heard of anyone in the entire industry who made a successful pitch at a Q&A, and you are unlikely to be the first. This is not your only opportunity. It is not an opportunity at all. But if you play your cards right, you *can* use the Q&A as an opportunity to meet people whom you can pitch later—at an appropriate time and place.

Filmmakers and talent will often stick around a bit after the Q&A to talk to people in the audience. This can be a great time to make an approach. Generally speaking, you want to present yourself not as a layperson but as someone in the industry. (So put those cameras and action figures away!) If you asked a question earlier, now is a good time to parlay that into a conversation. Don't come on too strong—just ask a question, start a dialogue, be interesting.

If the talent is even remotely well known, they will usually have a publicist or handler with them. These people function as gatekeepers to the main attraction. Do not be afraid to approach them, but handle yourself professionally. Gatekeepers are trained to repel stalkers—so one, don't be a stalker, and two, don't act like one. Present yourself in a normal and professional manner if you want a chance to talk with the talent. But you don't need to be ashamed of wanting to make connections. People who participate in Q&As understand that attendees use them as networking and research opportunities, and they will be amenable as long as you seem genuine and not psycho.

Your best bet is to stand back and observe the situation first. Identify the main publicist or handler, and then promptly and quietly introduce yourself. Be polite and to the point with publicity people. They are very busy, and they don't need or want a long-winded explanation of why you're there. If you are part of the festival in any way, say so. Be sure to let them know that you loved the screening, and if you spoke up during the Q&A, remind them of your riveting question. Mention that you had one more question, and ask them to ask the talent for you—usually they will simply let you ask it yourself. You will look professional, and you might just get a one-on-one conversation with the talent or filmmaker. If not, you've still made contact with an important publicist or handler whom you may run into later.

If you do get to talk to the talent, use the same quick and polite approach. Be conversational. Talk clearly and confidently. Be enthusiastic, nice, and genuine. Remember, celebrities are just people like you who happen to have already become successful. If you treat them like normal people, they will repay you the favor. Putting them on some pedestal is just alienating.

Depending on the talent, you may be able to continue the conversation later. If you have hit it off with someone professionally, you are well within your rights to ask for contact information or to offer to take them out for coffee or lunch. But this must be handled carefully. You don't want to seem creepy or unhinged. Make it clear that you want to talk about an idea you have or to hear about their careers. You want to seem both fun and professional, but not chummy or parasitic or transactional.

There's nothing crazy or pushy about saying something like, "Hey, my friends and I just saw your film and we stayed for the Q&A. We're headed down the street to dinner. Would you like to join us and talk movies?"

Generally, this works best if the person is just a few rungs ahead of you on the career ladder. If you have yet to break into the industry, you are probably not going to persuade Woody Allen, Roman Polanski, or J.J. Abrams to get a coffee with you, but you might have luck with someone whose short was a finalist at SXSW. This person is more likely to say yes because it is more likely you will be able to help each other in the foreseeable future.

Even if someone is far more advanced in their career than you are, try not to act starstruck—even if you really are. Early in my career, I went to the opening night of a movie at a film festival. I ended up helping to close the bar above the theater with the team who put the movie together. Sitting across the bar was Francis Fisher, who was involved in the film. I was only about twenty-five and somewhat new to the industry. She had just been in *Titanic*, then the highest-grossing movie of all time. I felt understandably intimidated. But everyone there said she was laid-back and approachable, so I approached her.

In introducing myself, I complimented her performance in a very specific and thoughtful way. It's important to avoid giving generic compliments. Just telling someone you loved his or her performance in a film isn't very engaging. It's too easy for them to just say thank you, and for that to be the end of the conversation. If you give a specific compliment, it opens up the possibility of dialogue and discussion. So be creative and clever with your compliments and with any questions. You want your opening line to open the door for them to respond in an involved way that might be the beginning of a conversation, rather than just a simple thank-you.

The final thing to keep in mind about Q&As is that, with any luck, you will one day be in the position of giving them. So in addition to researching how to become a success, you're also taking a crash course into how to ultimately run your own Q&A once you've made it.

12

How to Hobnob at a Cocktail Party: There's No Such Thing as "Just Drinks" in Hollywood

THE PUBLIC has an image of Hollywood as a place where industry insiders attend glamorous rooftop cocktail parties at luxury hotels like the W. Such events are, in fact, frequent, and they can be rather glamorous. Cocktail parties are ubiquitous in the entertainment industry. But if you think these functions are all about partying and enjoying the high life, think again. Amid the hustle and bustle and booze of your typical Hollywood cocktail party, deals are fermenting and connections forming. Professional relationships are being built and nurtured. Ideas are being tested and shopped around.

These kind of social events present opportunities that are valuable, if not downright essential, to your professional success. Tonight's casual acquaintance is tomorrow's industry contact. Late-night banter about ongoing projects can lead to new ideas for taglines, marketing campaigns, and casting offers. Offers are made with regularity at such events—as are the connections that eventually lead to offers. Idle conversation on a rooftop deck can lead to phone calls and an invitation to a pitch meeting during regular business hours.

Such connections can and do happen quickly, even subtly, over drinks, but these connections are neither simple nor haphazardly formed. Cocktail parties are not just another place where idle chatter might bloom into an exciting project. They are networking events, and intentionally so. When people gather for a cocktail party or a premiere's after-party or even an invite-only "after after-party" in the Hollywood Hills, they do so with the understanding that business will—not might, but *will*—mix with pleasure. Mixers are recognized as both social and professional gatherings.

The Hollywood pros know that deals can and are made over drinks. It behooves you to appreciate this, if you aspire to work in the industry. You'll need to learn how to navigate these frequent social occasions with aplomb or you'll risk leaving opportunities on the table. So be aware of opportunities and ready to act when they present themselves.

Years ago, I was hosting a charity event at a nightclub along with several competitors from two different studios. I spent the whole night making chitchat with potential donors. As the evening wound down, I found myself seated with a high-level executive from one of the other studios. We talked for a while and really hit it off. He ended up offering me a job right on the spot.

He made the offer by, and this is the honest truth, writing the salary figure down on a napkin and sliding it to me across the bar. I was stunned. For one, I thought this was something that only happened in the movies (it also happens in the movie business, apparently). Two, the number was far more than I was making at my then-current job. I played at nonchalance, but I'm sure my face belied my surprise.

Ultimately, I ended up declining the offer because I wasn't sure about the long-term opportunities. The salary was good, but the production studio in question was smaller than the major studio where I was working. I was afraid there would be less opportunity for advancement and development. This ended up being the right move. The other studio folded a few years later, and I'm still with the same company I was working with at the time.

For a long time, I kept that bar napkin as a reminder that things work very differently in the entertainment industry. Social events are places where business gets done, and that business can be conducted in a manner that is very impromptu and informal. This can work to your advantage if you get good at navigating cocktail parties and similar social functions.

Social settings have some advantages over traditional office settings. Business tends to be conducted less rigidly at a cocktail party, which means that you can really chart your own course. Meeting someone at a social event on a weeknight or a weekend also allows you to behave differently than you might in a strictly workday office setting. Often, you can act more naturally. You are better able to pace how a relationship unfolds. You can hold off on giving pitches and broaching business until the time is right. Social situations allow you to control the pace of professional interactions by taking advantage of the less rigid environment.

Just don't forget why you are there. If you plan on doing business at a party, avoid drinking too much. Alcohol can, of course, loosen some people up and ease anxieties, but it can also make you less sharp, so it's best not to use it as a crutch.

This should go without saying, but if you are at an event to network, don't drink so much that you get sloppy. Before attending a social event, ask yourself why you are there. Is it just to have a good time, or are you there to do business? There's nothing wrong with having fun, and you may find that opportunities arise even when you aren't looking for them. But if you have a professional mission, stick to it and you will probably find that you accomplish more than you might otherwise.

There can be drawbacks to doing business in nightclub and party settings, however. Occasionally you may run into the kind of person who takes the social setting as just that: a social setting. They may view what's said at a cocktail party as just talk, leading them to say things they don't really mean, especially if they have been drinking. You may run into people who will offer to read your pitch or tell you to come into the office sometime for a pitch meeting, but then never follow up with you.

This happens to everyone eventually, myself included, but as the above example about the bar-napkin job offer illustrates, real offers can be made at social events—so take them seriously and follow up. It's better to be disappointed by a false lead than to miss out on a genuine opportunity!

Knowing that there are people out there making false promises, I implore you—do not be one of them! It's unprofessional and shows that you don't understand how the entertainment industry works. In Hollywood, follow-through is everything. You want to be known as someone who says what they mean and does what they say. Even in social settings, you want to appear professional, genuine, and ambitious—so wear those qualities on your sleeve and keep your pet projects on the tip of your tongue. You want to always be prepared.

Networking Is an Art

There is an art and a craft to any business, and the business side of Hollywood is no different. Conversation, negotiation, and networking are arts that you need to understand and master. They take mindfulness and, of course, practice—just like filmmaking, acting, producing, marketing, or any other discipline.

Networking is the art of persuasion—you want to persuade people to like you. Luckily, many Hollywood types, especially actors, already possess this talent. The same qualities that appeal to broad audiences in theaters also impress individuals face-to-face. You don't need to turn up the charm to network success-fully—you don't want to appear false or sycophantic.

When approaching people, focus on clarity of message, confidence and delivery, and a hook to give the person you are speaking with something to hold on to. It's worth noting that the qualities that make for good networking are one and the same as those that make for a successful work of art. Much like successful art, people make a strong first impression when they impact with one lasting image. The finest piece of experimental material—whether it's a project, a piece of art, or a social interaction—will feel both meticulously planned and brilliantly off-the-cuff if it focuses on a single impression. This is also true of the first impressions that people make. People who make a lasting first impression generally evoke a staid centeredness, but they also have enough sureness of hand to improvise in conversation. They are responsive as well as calm and cool.

In Hollywood, the art of business is also the art of self-pres-ervation, so we eventually become masters of both. Interpersonal relationships are the lifeblood of the industry, and your career will rise or fall on your ability to cultivate relationships. For most people in Hollywood, much of this cultivation takes place at cocktail parties and other social events—not boardrooms, conference panels, and pitch meetings.

I met Edward James Olmos very early in my career, at a Dallas film festival where I was a sponsor. We first crossed paths at a cocktail party. I introduced myself and struck up a conversation about his film that was playing at the festival. We ran into each other several more times over the years, usually at cocktail parties. Let me stress, we're not necessarily heavy partiers or drinkers, but we do attend events like these. We are both in the industry and understand that business is conducted at these functions—we can't afford not to go.

I considered the day I introduced myself to Olmos a networking victory, and scored what I considered another victory later on when he asked me to please call him Eddie. I probably earned brownie points for remembering the film he was featuring at the festival where we met; it was a small project that I bet he himself barely remembers now that he's come so far in his career! But I showed him that I was paying attention. He remembered that I was a sponsor for the Dallas festival and asked me if I could help him with a Latin film festival he was working on. I ended up helping the festival recruit Latin executives and filmmakers, and I actually hosted an event to raise awareness for the festival. That event was—you guessed it—also a cocktail party.

Olmos and I aren't necessarily "friends," as we don't hang out or stay in touch, but we did forge a professional relationship that arose from a casual social interaction. And all I had to do was be friendly and confident at a cocktail party way back in the nineties.

The Elevator Speech—How to Do It and How Not to

Because people understand that cocktail parties are both social and business events, you *can* use them as a place to pitch ideas. There is absolutely no shame in attending a cocktail party with a project up your sleeve, but you can better your odds of finding receptive ears if you conduct yourself with a little (or a lot of) tact. There is a decorum to these things. You don't want to leave a social event without making your pitch, but it is far worse to create awkward situations that kill potential relationships. But don't be afraid to act when appropriate—having drinks with a colleague in Hollywood is never "just drinks." Everyone knows this and expects to be pitched at such events. But there's a right way to do this and a wrong way.

You want pitches to seem natural and off the cuff. Do not bring your script or any other written materials with you (doing so would seem both calculated and cheesy). You want to memorize your pitch and, when the time is right, toss it out casually. Timing and delivery are key. Make sure you have established a rapport first. Try to drop the pitch in a way that arises naturally from conversation. This is easiest when you have not memorized your pitch so much as internalized it. Be able to boil it down to one sentence, one paragraph, or whatever is appropriate to the moment.

Pitching means both having good ideas and being able to deliver them effectively. Lots of terrible ideas get passed around Hollywood, as do many inspired ones. But the general atmosphere is one where they all matter equally until they are produced. Every pitch has potential. And good delivery will help get good pitches noticed and, hopefully, produced.

Words are everything in Hollywood. Yes, yes…talk alone with no follow-through is cheap, but words are also the genesis of everything in Hollywood. Every product that has ever emerged from the industry started as words. Words that turned to actions and then to fully realized products—it happens every day here. It happens in splashy, impressive, and wide-reaching ways. It can seem grandiose. But it all starts with words. It starts with ideas and pitches.

Pitches and stories become your reality in the industry. In Hollywood, there is still a premium placed on the spoken and written word. What you say here gets you noticed. Idle talk at a cocktail party? No such thing. That's why you must be prepared—prepared to introduce yourself, prepared to mingle, prepared to pitch. No matter what you are doing, you are always pitching. You are pitching yourself and your projects every time you attend events like these—that's the nature of the industry.

13

Hollywood Charity Events: Give a Lot, Take a Lot

IN ADDITION to the many parties, screenings, and other social functions, the entertainment industry is full of charity organizations throwing charity events. These fund-raising events are often also social events, though, and make great networking opportunities. Recognize them as such. They are not only opportunities to make the world a better place and to feel better about yourself, but are also tools for advancing your career. Getting involved with industry-specific charities will put you into meaningful contact with other people in the entertainment business.

You want to get involved with a charity that is closely associated with the industry. For example, you may look for a charity that provides health insurance to struggling actors, or a group that supports young filmmakers, or a social justice charity that is supported by Hollywood insiders.

Don't be ashamed about helping a charity that also benefits you. These organizations are legitimate. That you also benefit from your association with them in no way detracts from their merit or the good work they (and now you) do. And you will feel good about yourself in a very personal way when you support a cause that you identify with on a personal level. Your genuine interest will be readily evident to others, and no one will question your intentions.

Different charity organizations align themselves with different areas of the industry. Some focus on the production side of the industry while others deal with distribution or marketing. Some align themselves with the exhibition side of the industry, providing space for public exhibitions and resources to young filmmakers. There are charities aligned with practically every aspect of the industry, so pick one that is most relevant to your specific career interests. If you're an up-and-coming filmmaker, get involved with a charity providing funding to up-and-coming filmmakers.

There are so many charities out there that I couldn't possibly name them all here. I am personally involved with the Variety Children's Charity and the Will Rogers Motion Picture Pioneers. I also really like the Fulfillment Fund and Inner-City Arts, both of which serve students from economically disadvantaged backgrounds. These are but a few of the charities you could get involved with—there are so many more out there. You can research relevant charities online. Their websites will tell you what the charity does and also what it needs—be it time or money. There's nothing wrong with giving money, but you should try to be as actively involved as possible. Often there will be the option to donate money to a specific event or project, and donating to these funds may allow you to meet people involved in those projects.

Don't worry if you are at the beginning of your career and short on cash. You can also give your time, which can be just as valuable and allows you to be directly involved with the charity.

Volunteering is a good way to put in sustained face time and to meet other people in the industry.

Charities will often host fund-raising events such as galas and auctions. Tickets can be relatively expensive, but attending these events can be a good career move as they are attended by other people who support the charity. This means you'll have access to industry people in a friendly social environment. Bonus: You already have something to talk about—the charitable cause you share in common!

I regularly support a charity that hosts many of these kinds of events, and they can be a lot of fun. They host a pool tournament in Hollywood that is attended by hundreds of people every year, and they also hold auctions. Another charity I support hosts an annual poker tournament on the Paramount Studios lot that draws many industry insiders, including a good number of A-listers and executives.

If you can't afford tickets, you can often attend events by volunteering to help. And you can usually stay at the event after your shift is over. That said, the tickets for these smaller, less formal functions are relatively economic—usually in the twenty to sixty dollar range—and are a good investment. The connections you can make are invaluable. You can meet all kinds of people.

So go to these events and get involved with these organizations. You'll do good and feel good. You'll meet people with similar interests and goals. You may even learn something about yourself while helping others in need. Your career may benefit, too—and there's nothing wrong or shameful about that!

PART IV

Maintaining the Connections that Will Launch Your Career

14

Forging Relationships: It Starts with Lunch, but It Takes Longer than a Single Meeting to Make a Meaningful Relationship

CONTRARY TO popular opinion, the art of face-to-face conversation has not been made obsolete by smartphones and videoconferences. This is especially true in Hollywood, where "having lunch" almost always means "doing business." If you're not doing lunch, you're missing out on business opportunities. You wouldn't eschew the boardroom for a videoconference—neither should you ignore the grand Hollywood tradition that is lunch. It is a great venue for networking.

Just because business can be conducted from afar doesn't mean that it should be. Trust me: I understand the allure of dashing off an email. It's fast. It's easy. You don't have to endure awkward, drawn-out conversations. But you also have less opportunity to forge real and lasting connections with people. It is easy to overlook the importance of forging real human connections when we are so bogged down in our day-to-day work and personal lives. Connection starts with interaction, but *strong* connections require so much more than that.

Phone calls and email have their place in setting up meetings, distributing information, even for catching up with someone, but they are not the best tools for building relationships. Consider how often you roll your own calls, ignore long voicemails from cold calls or even friends, or get buried beneath a mountain of unread messages in your inbox. Newsflash: You're not the only one! Other people feel the same way about these impersonal communications. They're ceaseless. They seem like work. Lunch, on the other hand, is an enjoyable way to do business.

Long before the telephone came along, humans were connecting by taking meals together. There is a reason for this storied tradition: Face-to-face meetings of this type provide a pretext for spending extended time together. This reduces awkwardness and promotes intimacy. There's no pull to end the conversation. No worrying if the other person wants to leave—they want to eat and pay their bill first.

This kind of easy and extended proximity allows conversations to flow naturally. We tell funny stories, engage in venting sessions, and are more likely to speak more personally and openly than we would over the phone. Think about it: When a friend calls and starts ranting long and hard about a bad experience, the conversation can quickly become tedious. However, if the friend delivers the same rant over lunch, coffee, or drinks, that rant is more likely to expand into an open conversation, with the speaker less likely to appear self-involved.

The setting in which a conversation takes place makes a major difference in how someone comes off. Meeting face-to-face is more personal and fun and creates a stronger, lasting impression than phone calls or email. So get out and have lunch with people. Meet business and personal contacts in person.

Why lunch? Because it's an industry tradition. Because sitting at your desk all day is boring. They don't give out medals for working a twelve-hour day and taking lunch hunched over your workstation, yet I see colleagues doing this all the time. Let these people stay chained to their desks if they want, but don't make the same mistake. When you neglect lunch to sit at your desk, you are, by default, neglecting taking lunch with others.

"Doing lunch" is a critical tool for expanding and strengthening your network. You absolutely cannot have a successful career by staying put in the office. You may solidify your reputation as a stalwart workhorse, but this will only carry you so far. Hollywood is a business of relationships, and doing paperwork at your desk isn't going to help you meet people. Take care of office business, of course, but set aside at least sixty minutes of your day for networking. Go out and meet with an agent, a manager, or a potential client. Doing this over lunch allows you to make the most of your time. Think of it as the best kind of multitasking!

You want to work, and work hard, but connecting with people on a more personal level is what propels one forward in a people-centric industry. You can't forge a career by trolling Internet sites, sending shot-in-the-dark emails, and making cold calls. You have to go out there and meet people to make things happen.

I was once introduced to a person who had been laid off from his first job at a minor studio through no fault of his own. A nonprofit that connects economically disadvantaged people interested in entering the entertainment industry with Hollywood executives put us in touch, and I agreed to have lunch with him. During the hour we spent together at a local restaurant, it came out that, in addition to some freelance work he was doing, he had been volunteering to help with a BBC documentary. As it so happened, I knew someone at the BBC who was looking for experienced interns. I put them in touch.

It is unlikely that his BBC experience and my casual BBC contact would have come up in the course of a five- or ten-minute phone conversation. It was the relaxed and extended nature of doing lunch that allowed for this to come up naturally. You will be hard-pressed to get sixty minutes to talk with someone one-on-one outside of the pretense of lunch, which is precisely why lunch is such a great networking tool.

Once you get the lunch date, do your homework. Those sixty minutes can be brutally awkward if you don't come well prepared and ready to talk. You don't want to just sit there staring at each other from across the table for an hour. Think about conversation topics beforehand, things you have in common, and subjects you could broach. You want the conversation to unfold naturally, but it helps if you have an idea of what you are going to talk about.

Making the *Right* Connections

By now I have probably hammered home the point that Hollywood is an industry driven by relationships. Careers are made by networking, which means that developing and maintaining a strong social circle will be key to your success. But not just any social circle will do. You need the right peer group. Peers should be people with whom you share similar goals and professional interests. If your social circle isn't supporting your dream, you need to find a peer group that will.

I am not telling you to dump all of your old college buddies, but you do want to be spending the majority of your time with people in or adjacent to the industry.

Ask yourself these two questions: Is my network made up of people who are going to help me get where I want to be? Am I making the most of my professional network? If the answer to both of these questions is not an emphatic yes, you need to start cultivating the right relationships.

Early on, I built a great support network that buoyed my career. Several of my friends had good jobs in the entertainment industry, or in adjacent industries like finance. We spent a lot of time together—sometimes up to seven nights a week! These nights resulted in the occasional imprudent hangover, but they also resulted in a lot of strong relationships in the industry. I am convinced that this helped propel me to where I am today.

Building strong relationships with industry professionals and associates helps create solid, lasting professional bonds between people. Relationships like these don't just matter, they are critical to professional success. While talent gets rewarded in Hollywood, the industry is hardly a strict meritocracy. Maintaining strong relationships could mean the difference between closing at a major pitch meeting or bombing with a world-class producer. Individuals who thrive in this business don't have a bunch of tricks up their sleeves. They have simply mastered effective communication and negotiation skills. They cultivated people skills and put them to use building networks that got them where they wanted to be.

When it comes to networking, you want to cast your net wide. Don't fall into the trap of thinking that only certain kinds of Hollywood insiders matter. You don't have to always be on the hunt for a celebrity run-in or chasing down top executives at top studios. Beyond glamorous actors and big-shot producers, there are many other people in the industry who can help you.

Practically anyone in the industry can be an asset to your social network. Meet everyone that you can and learn to enjoy doing so. I love making small talk with receptionists, assistants, and junior executives, for example. Not only are they industry gatekeepers, but they tend to be more approachable. They have a lot of the same interests and goals that you do, and you should engage them. And remember: While they may not be high-powered *now*, they might be *later*. Industries promote from within, and today's gatekeeper may hold the keys to the kingdom tomorrow.

Making First Contact

For many of us, reaching out is the hardest part of expanding our social network. That initial contact with a new person is hard for everyone, but it can be even harder for introverts. No matter your personality type, you *can* overcome fear of social interaction and learn to appear (if not actually be) comfortable approaching people. As with all things, practice makes perfect.

Try not to stress out unduly about making that first approach. You only have to do this once for each contact, and things get easier from that point on. Once you have reached out to someone, you will never have to cold-call them for the first time again! Approach the first interaction as you would removing a bandage—do it quickly and it'll be over before you know it.

When making the first move, so to speak, introduce yourself but don't make the mistake of talking too much about yourself and your needs. Get to know the person you are meeting. Ask them questions. Show a genuine interest in them and their needs.

Don't worry about appearing overeager. Reaching out for the first time sends an important message: that you care about your business and are interested in forming a mutually beneficial professional relationship. There's no reason to feel inherently awkward about that.

Be friendly, open, and inviting to new acquaintances you make in person. If you meet someone at an event and would like to get to know them better, exchange business cards or contact information. Do not let the contact go cold. Arrange something low-key, like a lunch meeting, within a week. Depending on the nature of the relationship, it might make sense to attend an industry event such as a screening or even just a movie together. This can sometimes lower the pressure to "perform" the first time you meet.

Once you have made first contact, always follow up. Continue to do so over the long haul of a relationship, for as long as you want to maintain that relationship. You may not always have much to offer in terms of proposals, pitches, ideas, or alliances, but that is no reason not to keep in touch. You never know when you may need your contact's services or help, or when they may need yours. And it's a lot easier to draw on someone for support when you have been there for them all along. Strong relationships require ongoing maintenance.

Be consistent and dependable and stay true to your word. In the long run, you will be glad you did. If you arrange a deal or schedule a meeting, honor your side of the arrangement. This is just good manners and professionalism, and your consistency of character will allow you to garner trust and respect from your colleagues.

Make the Most of Chance Encounters

Many relationships—maybe most—start as chance encounters. Chance encounters are random by definition, but the law of averages dictates that such opportunities will appear regularly as long as you put yourself in places and situations where they are likely to happen. In order to maximize opportunities to meet people, you should be doing just that.

I advise people to "always take the meeting." Always. Even if it is last-minute or inconvenient. If an event seems even tangentially related to the entertainment industry and you are still trying to break in, then *take the meeting!* You never know who you'll meet.

Very early in my career, after *Lights Out* had fallen apart but before I graduated from college, I was interning with a small direct-marketing consultancy. At the end of the semester, I stopped by the office to pick up my last mileage check, which I was going to use to make it back to my parent's house for the summer. It was maybe fifty dollars, but that was a bounty to a twenty-year-old college student in the eighties.

I showed up at the office with my luggage packed and in the trunk. My boss was in the back room. Along with my check, he handed me an invitation to a convention that was going on that very day. He couldn't make it due to other commitments. "I thought maybe you'd be interested," he said.

I wasn't all that interested. It was a convention for marketing professionals who specialized in selling ad time for cable television. If my internship here had taught me one thing, it was that I didn't want to work in advertising.

"Could be good for you," he said.

In the end, I did go. And here is why. First, I was going to be driving directly past the convention on my way out of town. Second, it was at Southfork Ranch, which is where the iconic eighties television show *Dallas* was filmed, and I thought it might be a nice chance to see a piece of television history. I dug out some khakis, a polo shirt, and a tie from the trunk of my car and headed over. I didn't know anyone there. A lot of the attendees were older, established professionals, and as a twenty-year-old student, I was honored when many of them asked to trade business cards. I didn't pursue advertising sales upon graduation, but if I had, the contacts I made there would have proven useful.

I think of my trip to Southfork Ranch as emblematic of the kind of spontaneous networking event that you shouldn't turn down just because it seems too spur-of-the-moment or inconvenient. When you're just starting out, you don't know exactly what sector of the industry you'll end up in, so you have to be ready to take advantage of these kinds of opportunities. Be ready for the chance encounter. Be open to surprise networking events. Be prepared to seize upon not just opportunity but the *possibility* of opportunity.

But What Can *I* Do for *You*?

Don't be the kind of person who takes without giving. When opportunities arise for you to help others with their careers—and they will—seize them with the same enthusiasm you invest in your search for personal opportunities. More often than not, your kindness will be reciprocated. You don't need to do things tit-for-tat. On the contrary, be selfless and generous, and people will show you the same kindness. We all want to be around genuine, generous, and kind people; be those things and your social network will expand far more easily.

I recently had a meeting with a woman struggling to break into the industry. She had tried networking and setting up meetings but was having a hard time finding employment. She had done some internships and some volunteering and had worked temp positions at Hollywood companies with the right names and addresses, but she hadn't been able to lock down that first entry-level position that would keep her in the game.

A friend of mine, who knows that my new company, Your Hollywood Pro, works with people trying to break into the entertainment industry, asked if I would give her some pointers. I invited her to lunch at the studio.

The moment the woman stepped into my office, I could see the problem—literally *see*. She had the wrong look. For better or worse, a certain style prevails in Hollywood, and this woman had not cultivated it. It wasn't about having good looks. It was about having the right look, the look that signaled that she understood the industry. Her dress and bearing were all off.

I mean no disrespect when I say that her outfit was more akin to what a waiter at an upscale steakhouse would wear than to the attire of an entertainment-industry professional. White shirt, black pants, and a wide tie—none of it fit well, and none of it was flattering. Certainly none of it was the proper couture for a lunch meeting with a Hollywood executive at a major studio. And yet, here she was!

The outfit indeed turned out to be the uniform she wore to her waitressing job at an upscale steakhouse—it was probably the nicest thing she owned. I do not tell this story to mock her, nor did I mock her at the time. I tried to be gentle and straightforward about advice that would help her break into the industry, carefully slipping some fashion suggestions into the conversation in the most diplomatic way possible. She took the hint, and while she may have been a little embarrassed at first, she thanked me profusely for being honest with her. I gave her tips on how to score nice clothes on the cheap from online auctions, store closeouts, and the like.

At the end of our meeting, she asked me a question. "Sorry," she fumbled. "I don't mean to be ungrateful, but why are you helping me so much?"

Her question made me feel awkward, but the answer was that I was helping her simply because I could. I truly believe in good karma—and not in some mystical way. When you show people goodwill, they return it in kind. I was giving her advice because I could, and because she needed it, and because I wished that someone had given *me* that kind of advice outright.

Early in my career, I interviewed for a casting assistant position on a TV show. I normally wore suits to my interviews, but it was cold outside and I decided to wear a nice sweater instead. People dress casually on sets and at production offices, and I thought it would be a nice touch to "look the part" of a casting assistant.

When I didn't get a callback even though I thought I'd nailed the interview, I broached the subject to the person who'd recommended me for the job when we bumped into each other at an event.

"What went wrong?" I asked.

"Did you wear a sweater to the interview?"

"Yeah. So?"

"Well…"

Apparently, my interviewer had been offended by my failure to suit up. Casting assistants may not wear suits or ties—but interviewees at studios sure do.

If someone had given me the proper guidance in this scenario, maybe I would have gotten the job. That's why I am generous with my knowledge and contacts. I don't see any reason why others should have to make the same mistakes I did, and it makes me feel good when I can help people avoid them.

A generous approach to networking has paid off for me in spades, but that's not even the point. This isn't a power play. I don't expect reciprocation, though I often get it. I won't lie: There are benefits to having helped out someone who later becomes influential in the industry. But the point is to be generous and to be yourself and to foster the kind of professional community you want to be a part of.

15

Do They Have Your Back, or Just a Knife in Your Back? How to Tell Who Is Supportive in Your Life and Career and Who Isn't

WHILE HOLLYWOOD is an industry driven by relationships, it is an unfortunate truth that not all relationships will be beneficial to your career. In the entertainment business, perhaps more so than in any other industry, it is critical that you be able to differentiate between those relationships that will benefit you and those that will hinder you.

In order to succeed in this industry, you will need to develop good intuition about people's true intentions. You need to be able to tell who is and who isn't really on your side. These kinds of judgment calls take practice, along with an understanding of the industry and what motivates people. Discerning between positive relationships and negative relationships is not always the straightforward proposition it may seem, and you may be surprised at some of the advice in this chapter.

For example, you may assume that your agent, whom you are paying to represent you, has your best interest at heart. This isn't always the case. You can't assume that someone is putting your interests first just because it is ostensibly their job to do so. You might reasonably assume that your agent, manager, or publicist will always put your career goals first, but this actually defies the laws of business. These people are businesspeople first and foremost, and they must put their business interests before the interests of any one individual client.

These people can certainly help you, and often will, but they do so for their own purposes. An agent will go out of their way to help you only if doing so profits their agency. To put it plainly: Agents are always trying to drum up business and publicity for their clients, but they have many clients and you may not always be their top priority. A big-shot agent is likely to prioritize big-shot clients who make more money.

You shouldn't feel married to your agent, manager, or publicist—they probably don't feel married to you. You are business partners, not life partners. If you get a better offer from another agent, or feel that another agent better meets your needs, feel free to consider jumping ship. The same applies to managers, publicists, and anyone else you are paying to pursue your interests. Personal relationships matter, but at the end of the day, these are professional relationships with real business repercussions. Just as an agent may sever ties with you, you may do so with them—it's just business, and no one should take it too personally.

I once landed a pitch meeting with Syfy (then called the Sci-Fi Channel) for an idea I had for a *Jeopardy*-style game show with a science-fiction, fantasy, and "geek culture" theme. The show was originally called *Fanboy Face-Off*, though I later changed the name to *I'm Your Number One Fan*.

My agent put me in touch with an agent who represented nonscripted material and, thus, would be better positioned to sell the show. This new agent was very positive on the phone and showed up to the pitch meeting pumped about the project.

He was enthusiastic and pushed hard for the show. After the meeting, he pulled me aside. He said that if it didn't work out with Syfy, he would get me in front of "this" network and "that" network until the idea sold.

Well, Syfy didn't work out. I got a call from the network, saying they had passed. From that moment on, I never heard from this new agent again. He didn't even bother to discuss Syfy with me and wouldn't return any of my calls or emails.

This is not the kind of agent you want to work with. Even if he had eventually called me back, I wouldn't have worked with him. Unscrupulous people will just drag you down. I don't blame him for dropping me as a client, but I do blame him for blowing me off.

There are two lessons to learn here. First, agents are guaranteed to want to help you only so far as it furthers their own interests. Second, "professionals" who don't display basic respect and professionalism should be avoided.

Do You Even Need an Agent? Yes and No.

Agents fulfill a very important role in connecting producers with talent. I would go so far as to say that agents might be an absolute necessity. But that doesn't mean you need one right away. There's no reason to seek out an agent before you need one. And, conversely, if you cannot find an agent, there is a good chance you don't need one yet.

If you are truly at a point in your career when you need an agent, finding one won't be difficult. Agents are there to make a profit off of selling your work or talent. If you have something salable, they will want to sell it for you. (If you don't have anything ready for the market, you will not be able to find a good agent, nor will you have any real need for one.)

If you can get pitch meetings, auditions, or properties on your own, you will be able to get an agent. You just need to show them that they have an opportunity to make a percentage of your money. Start making it on your own, and they will flock to you. But they will only come out of the woodwork once you really need them.

All of which goes to show that you need to put yourself and your work out there in order to find an agent. If you can't find one quickly, stop trying and get back to working on your product. The problem isn't that you don't have an agent. It's that you're not ready for one. It's tempting to think of agents as gatekeepers when you are on the outside looking in, but anyone who is already in the industry knows that agents are often great allies and partners. They aren't locking you out. They want to find fresh talent. That is their very job!

Don't turn down an agent if you can get one, of course. A lot of the major studios aren't too keen on accepting unsolicited material, both for legal reasons and because they want to look at talent and material that has already been vetted by people they know—agents. Studios often take a closer look at talent signed with a major agency for this one reason: You have already passed through a significant hoop in getting an agent.

If you don't have an agent, work on your product until you find one. I firmly believe that, at the end of the day, good work finds a home. If your content is good, if you have real talent and you remain persistent, you're going to be able to figure out a way to make it no matter what. No agent is going to turn you away if someone is willing to buy your property or cast you in a big movie. Get better, make those things happen, and the agent/publicist/manager "problem" will work itself out.

Lots of actors, producers, and directors don't even use agents these days. Often managers will take on the agent role, and sometimes people simply hire lawyers to negotiate deals as they come up.

Whichever route you take, realize that agents are a means to an end, not a goal in and of themselves. If you don't have the content to get the job, no agent is going to be able to help you. Remember: Content is king. Improve your product to the point where it becomes salable, and you'll have no problem finding someone to sell it for you—and scoop a percentage off the top!

Don't Make Potential Friends into New Enemies

Contrary to how Hollywood is often portrayed in the movies, we are not all cutthroat actors and jealous screenwriters bent on seeing our peers succumb to failure. Sure, there will always be the bad seeds, negative attitudes, and small-minded people—they exist in every industry, and you should learn to recognize them—but most people in Hollywood genuinely love seeing someone they know and respect make it big. They recognize that a rising tide lifts all boats.

Do not underestimate the support that your industry peers can provide. They can help you improve your craft, get better gigs, meet important people, and much, much more. Don't be deterred by jealousy or a fear of being undermined or sabotaged by members of your social network. You can't afford to cut off contacts for petty reasons like jealousy and fear. Networking snowballs; The more people you know, the broader your opportunity for future networking. Cutting people off has an exponentially detrimental effect on the size of your support network.

Show-Biz Acumen: Sniffing Out the Epic Fakes and Epic Flakes

Even though most people in Hollywood are generally kind and noble, there are exceptions to the rule. Let's talk about those bad seeds.

Earlier in this book, we talked about avoiding negative people, the types of people who bring you down. But you also want to avoid those who simply don't have your best interests at heart. This is another kind of negativity, one that arises from fear and jealousy.

Differentiating between those who do and don't have your best interests at heart is a large part of good show-biz acumen. I use a few litmus tests when trying to assess someone's intentions regarding our relationship. Think of these not as solid proof, but rather as red flags.

First, ask yourself: Does this person seem genuine? It is hard to fake sincerity over the long run. If you feel like someone is being disingenuous, they probably are. I give people the benefit of any doubt, but I also trust my gut. If I am getting a bad feeling from a person, I won't necessarily write them off, but I will monitor our relationship carefully until I feel confident in their good intentions and goodwill.

Second, ask yourself whether this person has been honest with you. Be wary of yes-men. You want the people in your network to actually listen to what you say and offer real feedback and advice rather than simply placating you. You want people to give it to you straight, not tell you want they think you want to hear (which they are often wrong about anyway). People who have your best interest at heart will not lie or bend the truth for their own ends. Peers who appease you at the expense of candidness may not have your best interest in mind. They may not understand just how important your career goals are to you, or they may not care. Either way, they are doing you no favors.

Third, ask yourself whether this person consistently upholds their end of the relationship bargain. If someone only calls you when they need something and always has an excuse for why they can't do you a favor when you need help, they may be using you. Give people the benefit of the doubt, but within reason. If someone cancels on you a few times, they may genuinely be busy, but if they make a habit of canceling, chances are they aren't trying or just don't care.

People who consistently behave in this way are epic flakes or epic fakes, or both. You need not waste your time on people who don't respect you—you have nothing to gain from them, professionally, socially, or emotionally. (And trust me, they will try your emotions as much as your patience!)

I once knew an agent at a top talent agency in Beverly Hills. He contacted me very rarely and only when he wanted something from me. I tried my hardest to keep my relationship with this person stoked, but he didn't make it easy on me. On multiple occasions, I set up dinner engagements with him only to have him cancel at the last moment. It's not like I didn't make it easy on him—I always arranged to meet near his home in east Hollywood. Still, he canceled on me every time, usually at the last minute, offering some thin excuse about why he couldn't make it. "Oh, that was *this* Sunday?" he would say after ignoring my calls for a half hour.

There are certainly advantages to keeping such a person at arm's length. There may come a time when you need them for something. But people who only pop up when they need favors tend not to be so good at returning those favors. They always have some excuse for why they can't help you with what you need.

I eventually collapsed my relationship with the agent—even though, as an agent at one of the top agencies, he was something of a powerful person in the epicenter of Hollywood. I didn't sever ties, but I stopped expending effort on the relationship. There was no reason for me to go out of my way when he consistently took without giving. It was clear that his relationship with me was insincere and exploitative. Be careful of people like this. Don't let them waste time or take up resources you could expend on yourself or, better yet, on more considerate contacts! (Before you sever ties, though, consider handing them a copy of this book, dog-eared to this particular chapter!)

16

You Don't Have to Stoke the Fires of Every Single Relationship: It's Okay to Let Some Relationships Go Cold

As IMPORTANT as it is to build your social network, you can, and sometimes should, let certain relationships in your network go cold. This may apply to the egregious fakes or flakes we discussed in the last chapter, but it may simply be a contact or acquaintance with whom you have no reason to stay in close touch.

You want to build the largest network you can manage successfully—the operative word here being *manage*. Realistically, you can't become best friends with everyone you meet in the industry. Limitations on time will force you to choose which relationships are the most important and relevant. Focus the majority of your attention on the relationships that you get the most out of.

Relationships that you want to keep require ongoing maintenance, but there is nothing wrong with disconnecting from someone temporarily and then reconnecting later when the time is right. You may not be able to automatically and immediately reconnect with someone from your network after letting the relationship go cold, but, trust me, if you have a good business reason for reaching out to someone, you will have no problem reconnecting.

This assumes, of course, that you were on good terms when you drifted apart and that you have always treated that person with respect. Don't expect someone you have blown off in the past to welcome you with open arms. This is doubly true if you are reaching out to the other party for something that you need. If the person doesn't see any benefit in resuming the relationship, they may not be interested in a rekindling, especially if you have previously offended them.

But if you left on good terms, the relationship can usually be revived, though you may have to take things slowly at first. Relationships that have gone cold are more akin to charcoal grills than gas grills. You can't expect to flip a switch and watch them fire up. You have to take your time and allow the relationship to warm back up slowly.

It's a step-by-step process. Start with a phone call to ask for lunch or drinks. When you first meet, you probably don't want to ask for any big favors right away. Show interest. Reconnect. Truly focus on the relationship, not bringing up anything you may want from them unless you believe that what you want will also benefit them. (In that case, pitch it as a mutually beneficial proposal—a fine reason for reconnecting with someone out of the blue.)

Before you reconnect, make sure that you have a good reason for doing so. Just as not all relationships need to be maintained, not all relationships need to be reignited. If you parted ways because there was no reason to maintain a connection and nothing has since changed, there may very well be no reason to restart the relationship now.

It can be quite tempting to want to buff each relationship all day long. I understand the predilection. Over and over again in this book, I have told you to focus on building relationships, and you have probably heard similar advice from others. It is true that your connections can go cold over time if you don't stoke the fires. This is only natural. Given that you have limited time in this world, you are going to have to make peace with allowing some relationships to go cold.

Trying to resume a relationship that has run its course can sometimes result in awkward situations. Random attempts to reach out to old contacts can be oh-so-awkward precisely because they seem so random. If an attempt to reconnect feels like a stretch, you may find contact with the other party to be forced, stiff, and inorganic.

I once decided to reconnect with a friendly contact from my TV internship days, a well-known news anchor in the Los Angeles area. We hadn't talked for a few years since my internship. When I landed my first studio job, I reached out to him to catch up and fill him in on my life now that I was a bigger player in the industry.

I first reached out by phone and reminded him who I was. We chatted about some of our old jaunts and former colleagues. The call was brief. After that, I let the relationship run cold again.

I didn't reconnect with him for many more years. In all honesty, I didn't really need to reconnect, but having been swayed by so-called experts on the importance of maintaining business relationships, I found myself calling up old contacts imprudently. Around this time, I heard that my news anchor acquaintance was hosting a food drive for the local station where he worked. This seemed like a good time to reach out. I showed up with some canned goods for donation. He didn't remember me this time; it had been so many years. I reminded him about some of our stories and common friends and colleagues from the old days.

I could see a light go off in his head, a clear recognition, but he still seemed a little put off. And why wouldn't he? Who was this weird person standing in front of him with an armful of cans? Why was he here? The conversation was terribly awkward. It wasn't until we went to trade business cards that I realized I was still holding the cans. I dropped them into the bin, took his card, and scurried away as quickly as I could. Neither of us has reached out to the other since.

Afterwards, I wondered what went wrong. This guy is a great person. I like to think I'm not so terrible myself. The problem was that we didn't really have any reason to stay in touch. I had a stable career at a movie studio. He was a longtime television anchor. Our paths had diverged and were unlikely to intersect again. This was one of those cases where I didn't need to reach out to a connection, because there was no reason to do so. Doing so resulted in an awkward situation that could have been avoided.

Reconnections have to develop organically. That's not to say you don't need to actively pursue them—you do—but there often needs to be either a reason or a pretext for taking up someone's time. In my eagerness to rekindle a relationship that didn't need to be rekindled, I risked damaging that relationship. I didn't consider timing, the point of contact, or the reason for contact. It would have been better to wait until we next crossed paths, probably through work. Instead, I came off as unprofessional and put him in an awkward position. Some reconnections are better not made.

Some *are* better made though. An interesting fact about my news anchor acquaintance is that he now acts in movies, usually playing a news reporter. Perhaps one day our paths *will* cross again, this time with a purpose. I can't say for sure, but one thing I know is that he and I have maintained a strong rapport and mutual respect. The door is still open if we need to reach out again—but if I'd kept on reaching out to him for no reason, he might have chosen to close it. And I wouldn't blame him. No one wants to be annoyed regularly without reason!

• • •

Relationships are like candles. You can pull them out of a drawer and ignite them, and even years later they can still work just as easily. But though they are certain to light up, there is no use for a lit candle in the middle of a bright sunny day.

Afterword

On Milestones and Finish Lines: The Journey Never Ends

A FUNNY thing happened to me the other day, as I was nearing the end of my writing process with this book. I was having lunch with the former head of a major Hollywood studio. He had just been pushed out of his job through no fault of his own. (It's just one of the things that happens sometimes in Hollywood.) I didn't know him personally and was hesitant to go to this lunch, fearing the situation would be awkward given the unfortunate circumstances. I also had jitters about meeting such an influential person. What would I have to say to the former head of a studio?

But I agreed to go. We met in a small restaurant in Hollywood. Our conversation that day was frequently interrupted by people coming over to say hello and commiserate with him about what had happened. As someone who had run a major movie studio, he was definitely an industry heavyweight. Lots of people knew him in Hollywood, and even more wanted to know him. A half-dozen people came up to talk to him one by one—there should have been a reception line!

My back was to the door, which prevented me from seeing these people until they were already upon us. One of them had a beard, hat, and glasses. Through my peripheral vision, I thought he almost looked like Steven Spielberg...and then I realized that he didn't just look like Spielberg—he was Spielberg!

The man I was having lunch with waved and said hello to Spielberg, who asked how he was doing in light of what had transpired.

I was speechless—here was my childhood hero. My mind went reeling back to that day when I stood in the Radio Shack staring at the *Making of "Raiders of the Lost Ark"* documentary so many decades ago.

It was then that my lunch companion asked Spielberg if he knew me. Spielberg smiled and greeted me warmly, extending his hand.

"Always an honor," I said, which I meant more than anything I have ever uttered before in my life. Being introduced to Spielberg in this way was a dream come true.

Had I not gone out to lunch that day, I would never have had the opportunity to meet my childhood hero, the man whose work had inspired my entire career in the entertainment industry, in such an intimate setting. I was glad I had not let jitters or simple inertia keep me from coming. What a tragedy that would have been!

My meeting with Spielberg was important to me not just because I got to meet a giant celebrity whom I admired, but also because I suddenly felt like I had come full circle. It was if I had completed some leg of a life journey that started in Radio Shack with the documentary and had come to a climax that day at the restaurant. Meeting Spielberg was the culmination of my journey from a small-town boy in Kentucky with big Hollywood dreams to a true Hollywood professional, the kind of person who has casual run-ins with one of the greatest and most renowned auteurs of all time. It was the realization of a dream, or rather a symbol for the realization of many of my personal dreams.

I relate this story here not to boast. I tell it because I want the same thing for you, dear reader.

Throughout my career, I have tried to give back, to be generous, to help others get where they want to be. I am not special. I am merely someone who put in the necessary work and learned—the hard way—what it took to be successful. My genuine desire is that others not have to make the same mistakes I did. Everyone must work hard to be successful, but by learning from those with experience, we can avoid making certain mistakes ourselves.

Simply by making myself available to people at conferences and events, and in my day-to-day life, I've helped hundreds of aspiring filmmakers, Hollywood hopefuls and newbies, and even midcareer entertainment industry professionals get on the right path to making movies and showcasing their talent. This book, *Your Hollywood Pro*, and my company of the same name (YourHollywoodPro.com) are extensions of this mission.

There are a lot of exploitative services out there pretending to do what Your Hollywood Pro does—that's part of why I founded the company. These services will promise you the world. They will promise to polish your script until it is Hollywood-ready and even promise to sell it for you. They'll promise to make you a famous actor. They'll promise to land you an agent. And yet most of these companies are staffed by people with zero track record in the industry. They are happy to take your money and tell you, "Yeah, your script thing is great. You're going to be huge!"

Your Hollywood Pro won't promise you anything other than consultations with people who have actually worked in the industry, in most cases for twenty years or more. Our stable of professionals includes actors, producers, writers, and other industry folks who have succeeded in their field. Many have made millions in Hollywood and have received critical acclaim for their work and recognition within the industry.

I didn't found Your Hollywood Pro or write this book to make a quick buck. I am a studio executive, and I make my living working in the entertainment industry. The reason I started the company was to create a service that will set people up for success. My genuine mission is to show all of those who think they cannot make it in Hollywood that they really can—and how to go about doing so. No one can point you toward the one true path to success, because there is no one-size-fits-all journey, but I hope this book has helped you cultivate some of the practices that will pave the way to your own dreams.

Those practices are important. Success is not something you achieve—it's a way of being. And it never stops. There is always more to learn and do and observe.

Meeting Steven Spielberg was a milestone for me, but it was no finish line. I have so much more to cross off my list. Just watching Spielberg interact with that former studio head, I realized that there was still a long way I could travel in this industry if I stayed at it. Situations like these remind me how much there is for me to learn, how much there is for me to do.

It makes me want to be more vigilant and present in my life. It reminds me to stop, watch, listen, and learn. It reminds me to keep growing and pushing myself—to keep evolving.

In early 2013, I was starting to feel stuck in a rut despite having what I know is an enviable career in Hollywood. As fortunate as I was, I wanted to break out and do more. Specifically, I wanted to exercise my creative side.

I had pursued that dream throughout my career, but my track record in this area hadn't been stellar. I'd started one TV show that failed (*Lights Out*) and pitched another that hadn't gone anywhere (*Fanboy Face-Off*). I was reluctant to try again for fear of failure. At the risk of abusing the tree metaphors: I wanted to branch out, but I was scared to put myself back out on a limb.

I was so afraid, in fact, that I hesitated when a friend solicited my help in producing a Broadway production of *Macbeth*. I didn't know the first thing about putting on a Broadway show. I was scared of failing, and my self-esteem was shot. Maybe I was just meant to be an industry suit. I was good at being a suit. I enjoyed being a suit. Why try to be something I was not?

Around this time, I was calling home to Kentucky quite often to talk with my grandmother. She had recently suffered a broken hip that had immobilized her. On top of that, my grandfather had just passed away. She was alone and spending a lot of her time in hospitals, unable to get around without assistance. So I called her frequently to check in and keep her company.

We made a lot of small talk. During one conversation, I let slip that I was thinking of passing on the *Macbeth* production. Now my grandmother didn't really know anything about the industry, and I don't think she totally understood the production or my proposed role in it, but she had always been supportive of my dreams and career. She often took me to movies when I was younger and recognized my passion.

In light of this, she was dumbfounded that I would pass on such an opportunity. "You always wanted to produce things and be a part of Hollywood and this sort of thing. Why on earth would you *not* do it?" she asked.

I started to protest but then stopped. She was right. Why wouldn't I do it? I was letting my own fear and self-doubt get the best of me. "You're right," I said. "I should do it."

And I did. We put on the production. Alan Cumming starred as the eponymous tragic hero. The play enjoyed a great Broadway run at the Ethel Barrymore Theatre and received rave reviews. Cummings won a Broadway.com Audience Choice Award for Best Actor and the show took home Best Revival. It was a total success.

What I hadn't really expected was how the production would reignite not only my passion but also my career. Colleagues began taking me more seriously. People started reaching out to me as a producer. I had always been recognized as a studio executive with a strong career, but now I was being acknowledged on a creative level, too. My social network began expanding at an unprecedented clip, and things started happening for me again. Throughout all of this, I was reminded of the power of these relationships and just how critical they are to one's success in Hollywood.

As you know by now, I try to give back to the community whenever I can, especially to young people attempting to break into the industry. I regularly speak at college symposiums and networking events—whenever I'm asked, basically. Recognizing how important connections and access are in Hollywood, I understood that the gifts of networking and connections were the most useful things I could give back to people trying to make it in the industry. Your Hollywood Pro was a natural extension of this same mission.

I met many of the people who are working with me on Your Hollywood Pro through producing *Macbeth*. This is, in its own right, a testament to the power of networks, connections, and access. One meeting or conversation led to another and another, and I soon found myself at the center of a vibrant and accomplished group of people. I asked many of them to lend their time and expertise to Your Hollywood Pro in order to get the site going, and most were happy to oblige. They advised me. They gave time and resources. Some became "Pros" on the website. Collectively, they helped me launch what is fast becoming a powerful tool for helping people realize their Hollywood dreams.

Credit where credit is due: None of this would have happened if I hadn't taken my grandmother's advice to ignore my fears and follow my dreams. I still credit her with this breakthrough in my career and life. Sadly, she couldn't make it to see the play because she was bedridden from her hip fracture, from which she never recovered. But I was able to get her a signed playbill from the show—my father handed it to her in person right before she passed away—which meant a lot to her. I hope she knows what it meant to me.

Your Hollywood Pro is my attempt to keep growing and to help others do the same. The only end in life is death. There is always more to absorb and more to learn. Watching films is still my favorite pastime and education. On the shelves in my home office right now are hundreds of unwatched DVDs and Blu-rays. There are weeks of content waiting on my DVR, a whole library in my Netflix queue. This is all content I plan to consume and learn from. I want to absorb as much as I can.

I want to engage with people more, too. I want to attend more film festivals and do even more networking. I want to develop more and better relationships as both a mentor and a student. You never run out of ways to learn or reasons to engage. The more I know, the more I can impart to those I teach.

I have my own plans for the future as well. There are more childhood heroes to meet and more places to see. I would like to take part in all of the major film festivals, both here and abroad. I plan to produce and write more. I want to do more plays, more shorts, more features, and even another TV show—this time one that's a smashing success! I want to fulfill all of my dreams and then find new ones.

And I want the same thing for you.

CPSIA information can be obtained at www.ICGtesting.com
Printed in the USA
BVOW09*0802031114

373072BV00005B/6/P